Table of Contents

Chapter 1: Introduction to Rust...22

　1.1 The Origin and Philosophy of Rust..22

　　The Birth of Rust...22

　　Rust's Philosophy 22

　　Zero-Cost Abstractions..22

　　The Rust Community 22

　　Adopting Rust...23

　1.2 Key Features of Rust...23

　　1. Memory Safety 23

　　2. Ownership and Borrowing 23

　　3. Concurrency Without Data Races...24

　　4. Zero-Cost Abstractions..24

　　5. Pattern Matching...24

　　6. Ownership Guarantees...25

　1.3 Comparison with Other Programming Languages...25

　　1. Safety and Memory Management...25

　　2. Concurrency...25

　　3. Performance...26

　　4. Ecosystem and Libraries 26

　　5. Learning Curve...26

　　6. Web Development...26

　　7. Systems Programming..26

　　8. Community and Support 26

　1.4 Installing and Setting Up the Rust Environment...27

　　1. Installing Rust 27

　　2. Verifying the Installation...27

　　3. Setting Up a Rust Project...27

　　4. Understanding `Cargo.toml`..28

　　5. Building and Running Your Project 28

　　6. Exploring Rust Documentation 28

　　7. Integrated Development Environments (IDEs)...28

　1.5 Writing Your First Rust Program...29

1. Creating a New Rust Project 29

2. Editing the Main Source File 29

3. Building and Running the Program 29

4. Understanding the Code 30

5. Expanding Your Program...30

Chapter 2: Basic Concepts in Rust..31

2.1 Understanding Variables and Mutability...31

2.1.1 Variable Declaration and Initialization...31

2.1.2 Mutable and Immutable Variables...31

2.1.3 Shadowing Variables 31

2.1.4 Constants 32

2.1.5 Summary 32

2.2 Data Types and Structures...32

2.2.1 Scalar Types...32

2.2.2 Compound Types..32

2.2.3 Compound Data Structures..33

2.2.4 The `String` Type..33

2.2.5 Ownership and Data Types 34

2.3 Control Flow in Rust...34

2.3.1 Conditional Statements...34

2.3.2 Looping Constructs..35

2.3.3 Flow Control in Loops 36

2.3.4 The `return` Statement...36

2.4 Functions and Modular Programming...37

2.4.1 Function Definitions...37

2.4.2 Calling Functions 37

2.4.3 Function Parameters and Arguments 38

2.4.4 Function Return Values 38

2.4.5 Function Visibility 39

2.4.6 Function Overloading 39

2.4.7 Summary 40

2.5 Error Handling Basics 40

2.5.1 The `Result` Enum..40

2.5.2 Handling Errors with `match`..40

2.5.3 The `Option` Enum..41

2.5.4 Unwrapping Results and Options...41

2.5.5 Propagating Errors 42

2.5.6 Custom Error Types..42

2.5.7 Summary 43

Chapter 3: Advanced Data Types...44

3.1 Exploring Enums and Pattern Matching....................................44

3.1.1 Enumerations in Rust...44

3.1.2 Using Enums 44

3.1.3 Pattern Matching 44

3.1.4 Exhaustive Matching...45

3.1.5 Matching with Values 45

3.1.6 Using _ for Placeholder...45

3.1.7 Combining Patterns 46

3.1.8 Summary 46

3.2 Generics and Their Applications 46

3.2.1 Understanding Generics...46

3.2.2 Using Generics with Functions 47

3.2.3 Using Generics with Structs 47

3.2.4 Using Generics with Enums 48

3.2.5 Using Generics with Traits 48

3.2.6 Limiting Generics with Trait Bounds....................................48

3.2.7 Summary 49

3.3 Traits and Abstract Data Types 49

3.3.1 Defining Traits 49

3.3.2 Implementing Traits 49

3.3.3 Trait Bounds..50

3.3.4 Default Implementations 50

3.3.5 Multiple Trait Implementations...50

3.3.6 Trait Objects 51

3.3.7 Summary 51

3.4 Collections in Rust 52

3.4.1 Arrays 52

3.4.2 Vectors 52

3.4.3 Strings 52

3.4.4 Slices 53

3.4.5 HashMaps 53

3.4.6 Iterators..53

3.4.7 Summary 53

3.5 Smart Pointers and Memory Safety 54

3.5.1 The Box Smart Pointer 54

3.5.2 The Rc and Arc Smart Pointers...54

3.5.3 The RefCell Smart Pointer 54

3.5.4 The Mutex and RwLock Smart Pointers 55

3.5.5 The Drop Trait...55

3.5.6 Summary 55

Chapter 4: Ownership and Borrowing 57

4.1 The Ownership Model in Rust...57

4.1.1 Ownership Rules..57

4.1.2 Ownership and Variables..57

4.1.3 Ownership Transfer 57

4.1.4 Ownership and Functions...58

4.1.5 Borrowing..58

4.1.6 Ownership and Mutability..58

4.1.7 Ownership and Lifetimes 59

4.1.8 Summary 59

4.2 Borrowing and References 60

4.2.1 Mutable and Immutable References 60

4.2.2 Borrow Checker 60

4.2.3 Dangling References...61

4.2.4 References as Function Parameters..61

4.2.5 References in Structs 61

4.2.6 Summary 62

4.3 Lifetime Annotations...62

4.3.1 What Are Lifetimes?...62

4.3.2 Lifetime Annotations in Function Signatures 62

4.3.3 Lifetime Elision..63

4.3.4 Lifetime Bounds...63

4.3.5 Lifetime Annotations in Structs and Enums 63

4.3.6 Lifetime Bounds in Traits 64

4.3.7 Lifetime Annotations in Function Signatures 64

4.3.8 Lifetime Annotations in Struct and Enum Definitions 64

4.3.9 Summary 65

4.4 Understanding Memory Allocation 65

4.4.1 Stack and Heap 65

4.4.2 Ownership and Memory Allocation 65

4.4.3 Data Copies vs. Ownership Transfers 66

4.4.4 Clone Trait 66

4.4.5 Memory Leaks 66

4.4.6 Dangling Pointers 66

4.4.7 Summary 67

4.5 Ownership in Practice: Building Robust Applications 67

4.5.1 Memory Management 67

4.5.2 Error Handling 68

4.5.3 Design Patterns and Best Practices 69

4.5.4 Summary 69

Chapter 5: Concurrency in Rust 71

5.1 Introduction to Concurrency and Parallelism 71

5.1.1 What is Concurrency? 71

5.1.2 What is Parallelism? 71

5.1.3 Concurrency vs. Parallelism 71

5.1.4 Thread-Based Concurrency 72

5.1.5 Asynchronous Programming 72

5.1.6 Summary 72

5.2 Threads and Thread Safety 73

5.2.1 Creating Threads 73

5.2.2 Thread Communication 73

5.2.3 Thread Safety and Data Races 75

5.2.4 Thread Safety and Send/Sync Traits 75

5.2.5 Summary 75

5.3 Rust's Concurrency Guarantees 75

5.3.1 Ownership and Borrowing 75

5.3.2 Send and Sync Traits...76

5.3.3 The Send Trait and Concurrency...77

5.3.4 The Sync Trait and Concurrency 77

5.3.5 Summary...77

5.4 Asynchronous Programming in Rust...78

5.4.1 What is Asynchronous Programming?......................................78

5.4.2 Asynchronous Libraries in Rust...78

5.4.3 Benefits of Asynchronous Programming..................................79

5.4.4 `async`/`await` Syntax...79

5.4.5 Summary...80

5.5 Building Concurrent Applications in Rust.....................................80

5.5.1 Identifying Concurrent Tasks 80

5.5.2 Thread-Based Concurrency..80

5.5.3 Asynchronous Programming 80

5.5.4 Synchronization 81

5.5.5 Channels for Communication...81

5.5.6 Choosing the Right Concurrency Model 82

5.5.7 Summary...82

6.1 Advanced Error Handling Techniques...82

Result Combinators 83

Custom Error Types 84

Recoverable vs. Unrecoverable Errors...85

Summary 85

6.2 Using Rust's Debugging Tools 85

Printing Debug Information..85

Using the `dbg!` Macro..86

Debugging with `eprintln!` 86

Using the `RUST_LOG` Environment Variable 87

Using a Debugger..87

Summary 88

6.3 Writing Testable Code 88

Writing Unit Tests 88

Organizing Tests 89

Writing Integration Tests...89

Test Attributes and Features..90

Summary...91

6.4 Benchmarking and Performance Analysis....................................91

Benchmarking with `bencher`...91

Analyzing Benchmark Results...92

Profiling with `cargo flamegraph`..92

`cargo fmt` and Code Formatting...92

Profiling with `cargo-profiler`...93

Summary...93

6.5 Common Rust Programming Mistakes and Solutions..................93

1. Ownership and Borrowing Errors...93

2. Null Pointer Errors...94

3. Uninitialized Variables...94

4. Missing `Result` Handling...95

5. Incorrect Use of `unwrap`..95

6. Mutable Variables When Immutability Is Sufficient....................95

7. Inefficient String Manipulation...96

8. Unnecessary Cloning..96

9. Missing Documentation and Comments.......................................96

10. Ignoring Warnings...96

Chapter 7: Rust's Ecosystem and Tooling..97

7.1 Understanding Cargo and Crates..97

What is Cargo?...97

Crates in Rust..97

Creating a New Rust Project...97

Managing Dependencies with Cargo.toml..98

Building and Running a Rust Project..98

Publishing Your Crate...98

Conclusion...99

7.2 Managing Dependencies...99

Adding Dependencies..99

Specifying Version Constraints...100

Updating Dependencies...100

Locking Dependencies with Cargo.lock..100

Building and Managing Dependencies 100

Conclusion..101

7.3 Rust Documentation and Community Resources...101

Official Rust Documentation 101

Crates.io Documentation 102

Community-Driven Resources...102

Editor and IDE Integration 102

7.4 Integrating Rust with Other Languages...103

Foreign Function Interface (FFI)..103

Rust Bindings...103

Interoperability with C++..103

WebAssembly Integration 103

Python Integration 104

Node.js Integration..104

C# and .NET Integration 104

Conclusion...104

7.5 Building and Publishing Your Own Crate 104

Creating a New Crate...104

Structuring Your Crate 105

Writing Your Crate 105

Adding Dependencies 105

Building and Testing Your Crate 106

Publishing Your Crate 106

Versioning Your Crate..106

Conclusion...106

Chapter 8: Functional Programming in Rust...107

8.1 Principles of Functional Programming..107

Immutability 107

First-Class and Higher-Order Functions..107

Pure Functions 107

Immutable Data Structures 108

Pattern Matching..108

Conclusion...108

8.2 Iterators and Closures..108

Iterators in Rust..109

Closures in Rust..109

Chaining Iterators and Closures...109

Laziness and Evaluation 110

Conclusion..110

8.3 Functional Design Patterns..110

1. Map and Reduce 110

2. Pipe...110

3. Memoization...111

4. Currying and Partial Application..111

5. Monads 111

8.4 Functional Data Structures..112

1. Immutable Lists 112

2. Persistent Maps 112

3. Option and Result...113

4. Functional Queues 113

8.5 Leveraging Rust's Functional Features..114

1. First-Class Functions 114

2. Closures...115

3. Iterators 115

4. Pattern Matching..115

5. Immutability...115

Chapter 9: Rust for Web Development 117

9.1 Introduction to Web Assembly and Rust......................................117

What is WebAssembly (Wasm)? 117

Rust and WebAssembly...117

Getting Started with Rust and WebAssembly...............................118

9.2 Building Web Applications with Rust..119

Choosing a Web Framework..119

Dependency Management with Cargo...119

Handling HTTP Requests and Routes 120

Templating and Views 120

Database Integration..121

Frontend Development with Yew..121

9.3 Rust in Backend Development...122

Building HTTP Services..122

Managing Dependencies with Cargo 124

Database Integration..124

Middleware and Authentication..125

Testing and Deployment..125

9.4 Integrating Rust with JavaScript...126

WebAssembly and Rust..126

Using Rust in a Web Application 126

JavaScript Interoperability 127

Leveraging JavaScript Libraries 127

Node.js and Rust..127

9.5 Case Studies: Successful Rust Web Projects 128

1. Rocket: A Web Framework for Rust 128

2. Warp: Asynchronous Web Services 128

3. Actix: Actor-Based Framework..128

4. Parcel: Web Application Bundler 129

5. Sonic: Fast Search Server...129

Chapter 10: Cross-Platform Development with Rust...............................130

10.1 Rust on Different Operating Systems..130

Why Cross-Platform Development? 130

Rust for Cross-Platform Development..130

Cross-Platform Rust Tools 131

10.2 Rust on Different Operating Systems: A Practical Guide............132

Writing Cross-Platform Code..132

Using Cross-Platform Libraries 133

Cross-Compiling Rust Code 133

Conclusion...133

10.3 GUI Development with Rust: Building Cross-Platform Interfaces 134

Choosing a GUI Framework...134

Developing a Cross-Platform GUI Application 134

Considerations for Cross-Platform GUI Development........................135

10.4 Mobile Development with Rust: Building Cross-Platform Mobile Apps....................136

Mobile Development with Rust and Flutter 136

Building a Cross-Platform Mobile App with Rust and Flutter................................136

Considerations for Mobile Development in Rust................................137

10.5 Building Cross-Platform Applications with Rust................................138

1. Cross-Platform Development Frameworks................................138

2. Web-Based Cross-Platform Apps................................139

3. Mobile Cross-Platform Apps................................139

4. Game Development................................139

5. Desktop Applications................................140

6. Command-Line Tools................................140

Chapter 11: Rust for Systems Programming................................141

Section 11.1: Rust in Operating Systems Development................................141

The Advantages of Rust in OS Development................................141

Use Cases for Rust in OS Development................................141

Challenges and Considerations................................142

Section 11.2: Network Programming with Rust................................142

Building Network Servers................................142

Asynchronous Networking................................143

Protocol Parsing and Serialization................................144

Section 11.3: File System and I/O Operations................................144

Reading and Writing Files................................145

Directory Operations................................145

Standard Input and Output................................146

Section 11.4: Building Command-Line Tools................................146

Command-Line Argument Parsing................................146

Running External Commands................................147

Creating Interactive Tools................................148

Section 11.5: Rust in High-Performance Computing................................148

Performance and Safety................................148

Parallelism and Concurrency................................149

Interoperability................................149

SIMD and Vectorization................................149

GPU Programming................................149

Numerical Computing Libraries................................150

Chapter 12: Advanced Rust Programming Techniques................................151

Section 12.1: Macros and Metaprogramming 151

What Are Macros?...151

Macro Invocation 151

Code Generation 151

DRY (Don't Repeat Yourself) Principle..152

Challenges and Pitfalls 152

Section 12.2: Advanced Traits and Type Systems 152

Associated Types...152

Supertraits 153

Phantom Types 154

Advanced Type Constraints 154

Advanced Traits and Type System Summary...155

Section 12.3: Unsafe Rust for Low-Level Control 155

The "unsafe" Keyword 155

Unsafe Functions and Blocks 156

Unsafe Traits and Implementations 156

Safe Abstractions with Unsafe Code 157

Guidelines for Using "unsafe" 157

Section 12.4: Optimizing Rust Code..157

Profiling and Benchmarking 157

Data Structures and Algorithms..158

Profiling and Optimizing Hot Loops 158

Compiler Optimization Flags 158

Unsafe Code for Low-Level Optimization..158

Caching and Memoization 159

Avoiding Unnecessary Allocations 159

Parallelism and Concurrency...159

Section 12.5: Exploring Rust's Type System 159

Strong and Static Typing...160

Type Inference 160

Ownership and Borrowing 160

References and Borrowing 160

Enums and Pattern Matching 161

Traits and Polymorphism..161

Custom Types and Abstraction 162

Chapter 13: Rust for Game Development..162

Section 13.1: Introduction to Game Development with Rust.......................162

Section 13.2: Rust Game Engines and Frameworks 164

ggez 164

Amethyst..165

Bevy 166

Other Options 166

Section 13.3: Graphics Programming in Rust..167

Rendering with OpenGL and Vulkan 167

Graphics Shaders 168

2D and 3D Graphics 169

Section 13.4: Handling User Input and Events...169

Event Loop and Event Handling..169

Input Handling Abstractions..170

GUI Libraries...171

Section 13.5: Building a Simple Game in Rust..172

Game Development Libraries...172

Setting Up the Project 172

Creating a Game Loop 172

Adding Game Logic and Graphics 173

Conclusion...174

Chapter 14: Rust and Cryptography..175

Section 14.1: Cryptographic Concepts in Rust..175

What is Cryptography?...175

Cryptographic Primitives 175

Conclusion...176

Section 14.2: Implementing Encryption Algorithms in Rust....................177

Choosing the Right Algorithm 177

Using External Libraries 177

Implementing Custom Algorithms 178

Secure Key Management 178

Conclusion...178

Section 14.3: Rust in Blockchain and Cryptocurrency 178

13

Building Blockchain Protocols 179

Smart Contracts and dApps..179

Cryptocurrency Wallets and Tools...179

Security Auditing and Penetration Testing 179

Conclusion..179

Section 14.4: Secure Communication with Rust 180

Web Servers 180

Networking Protocols 180

Messaging Systems..180

Encryption and Authentication 180

Secure Coding Practices...180

Conclusion..181

Section 14.5: Building Cryptographically Secure Applications 181

Why Cryptographic Security Matters...181

Rust's Role in Cryptographic Security 181

Building Cryptographically Secure Applications 182

Conclusion..182

Chapter 15: Rust for Data Science and Machine Learning..183

Section 15.1: Rust in the World of Data Science..183

The Advantages of Using Rust in Data Science 183

Use Cases for Rust in Data Science...183

Challenges and Considerations...184

Conclusion..184

Section 15.2: Data Processing and Analysis in Rust 184

Reading and Parsing Data 185

Data Transformation and Cleaning..185

Numerical Computing...186

Concurrency for Data Processing 186

Visualization and Plotting...187

Section 15.3: Machine Learning Libraries in Rust..187

1. ndarray and nalgebra...187

2. tangram..187

3. rust-learn 188

4. tract 189

Section 15.4: Building Predictive Models with Rust..189

1. Data Preparation 189

2. Model Selection...189

3. Training the Model 189

4. Model Evaluation 190

5. Hyperparameter Tuning..190

6. Deployment 190

7. Monitoring and Maintenance..190

Section 15.5: Case Studies: Rust in Data Intensive Applications 191

1. Servo: A Modern Web Browser Engine 191

2. Tantivy: A Full-Text Search Engine Library 191

3. DataFusion: A Distributed SQL Query Engine 191

4. Parquet: A Columnar Storage Format...191

5. Heim: A Cross-Platform System Information Library..192

6. Polars: A Data Manipulation and Analysis Library...192

Chapter 16: Scalability and Performance in Rust...193

Section 16.1: Writing High-Performance Rust Code 193

Performance Considerations in Rust...193

Profiling and Benchmarking...193

Writing Efficient Algorithms...193

Memory Management and Optimization...194

Profiling Rust Code..194

SIMD (Single Instruction, Multiple Data)..194

Parallelism and Concurrency..194

Load Balancing and High Availability 194

Real-World Case Studies..194

Section 16.2: Memory Management and Optimization 194

Stack vs. Heap..195

Lifetimes and Borrowing..195

Reusing Memory 195

Copy vs. Clone...195

Rust's Allocator API 196

Cache-Friendly Data Structures...196

Section 16.3: Scalable System Architectures 196

Parallelism and Concurrency...197

Asynchronous Programming...197

Message Passing..197

Load Balancing and High Availability 198

Horizontal Scaling..198

Microservices and Containerization..198

Section 16.4: Load Balancing and High Availability 199

Load Balancing..199

High Availability 200

Distributed Systems and Rust..200

Section 16.5: Case Studies: Performance Optimization in Rust 201

Case Study 1: Servo Browser Engine...201

Case Study 2: Tokio Asynchronous Runtime 201

Case Study 3: Data Serialization with Serde...201

Case Study 4: Rust in Game Development 202

Case Study 5: Rust in Cryptocurrency 202

Chapter 17: Rust in the Enterprise 203

Section 17.1: Adopting Rust in Large-Scale Projects..............................203

The Rust Safety Promise..203

Performance at Scale...203

Productivity and Maintainability 203

Real-World Examples...203

Overcoming Challenges...204

Section 17.2: Rust for Enterprise Security...204

Memory Safety and Security 204

Protection Against Data Races 205

Secure by Default..205

Third-Party Audits 205

Cryptography and Secure Communication..205

Secure Enterprise Solutions in Rust...205

Section 17.3: Building Microservices with Rust.....................................206

Performance and Efficiency 206

Safety and Reliability..206

Concurrency and Parallelism...206

Ecosystem and Libraries...206

Containerization and Deployment 207

Cross-Platform Compatibility...207

Section 17.4: Rust in Cloud Computing...207

Serverless Computing..207

Containers and Orchestration 208

Cloud-Native Databases 208

Cloud Infrastructure as Code..208

Cloud-Native Monitoring and Observability 208

Section 17.5: Case Studies: Rust in Corporate Environments 209

Dropbox: Rewriting Critical Components for Safety and Performance 209

Mozilla: Building a More Secure Web Browser 209

Cloudflare: Leveraging Rust for Networking and Security..209

Microsoft: Utilizing Rust in Azure IoT Edge 210

Figma: Empowering Design Collaboration with Rust..210

Chapter 18: Future Trends and Directions in Rust...211

Section 18.1: Rust's Roadmap and Future Developments 211

1. Stabilization of Features 211

2. Ergonomics and Developer Experience 211

3. Async/Await and Concurrency 211

4. Wider Adoption in Systems and Web Development...211

5. Expansion of the Rust Ecosystem 211

6. Integration with Other Languages..212

7. Rust in Education 212

8. Community Involvement..212

Section 18.2: Emerging Domains and Applications for Rust 212

1. WebAssembly (Wasm) Development 212

2. Blockchain and Cryptocurrency 212

3. Embedded Systems and IoT..213

4. Game Development..213

5. Machine Learning and Data Science 213

6. Cloud Computing...213

7. Networking and Network Services...213

8. Quantum Computing 213

Section 18.3: Rust in the Open Source Community 214

    1. Open Source Roots..214

    2. Package Management with Cargo..214

    3. Contributions to the Wider Open Source Ecosystem 214

    4. Community-Driven Development..214

    5. Education and Outreach..214

    6. Cross-Project Collaboration 215

    7. Security and Trust 215

    8. Community Engagement...215

Section 18.4: Challenges and Opportunities for Rust 215

    1. Learning Curve...215

    2. Library Ecosystem..215

    3. Adoption in Legacy Codebases...216

    4. Tooling..216

    5. Cross-Platform Development 216

    6. Integration with Other Languages..216

    7. Security and Trust 216

    8. Community Growth...216

    9. Rust in Emerging Domains...217

    10. Educational Initiatives 217

Section 18.5: Preparing for the Future with Rust......................................217

    1. Continuous Learning 217

    2. Contribute to Open Source Projects..217

    3. Explore Emerging Domains..217

    4. Diversify Your Skill Set 218

    5. Participate in the Rust Community 218

    6. Stay Informed About Rust's Roadmap...218

    7. Experiment and Innovate...218

    8. Mentorship and Teaching..218

    9. Adapt to Industry Trends 218

    10. Remain Adaptable..218

Chapter 19: Real-World Rust Projects...220

Section 19.1: Analyzing Open-Source Rust Projects..................................220

    Finding Open-Source Rust Projects 220

Evaluating Project Relevance 220

Cloning and Exploring Repositories 220

Reading Documentation 220

Analyzing Code Structure..220

Studying Contributions and Pull Requests 220

Running Tests and Benchmarks..221

Contributing to Projects..221

Tools for Analyzing Rust Projects..221

Learning from Diverse Projects..221

Section 19.2: From Concept to Code: Developing a Rust Project.............221

Defining Your Project...221

Planning and Design 222

Choosing Dependencies 222

Setting Up the Development Environment..222

Writing Code 222

Version Control...222

Testing 222

Continuous Integration 223

Documentation 223

Community and Collaboration 223

Security and Maintenance...223

Deployment and Distribution 223

Monitoring and Feedback 223

Section 19.3: Project Management for Rust Development........................223

Choosing a Project Management Methodology 224

Setting Clear Objectives 224

Creating a Project Plan 224

Managing Resources..224

Communication and Collaboration 224

Risk Management 224

Task Tracking and Progress Monitoring 224

Agile Development Practices 225

Documentation 225

Quality Assurance..225

Change Management..225

Project Closure..225

Section 19.4: Rust in Production: Success Stories...225

1. Dropbox...225

2. Mozilla...226

3. Cloudflare..226

4. Parity Technologies..226

5. Microsoft..226

6. Figma..226

7. Discord...226

Section 19.5: Learning from Real-World Rust Applications 227

1. Code Readability..227

2. Safety and Concurrency 227

3. Error Handling 227

4. Testing and Documentation 227

5. Dependency Management..228

6. Design Patterns and Architectural Choices 228

7. Performance Optimization...228

8. Community and Collaboration 228

Chapter 20: Concluding Rust Journey...229

Section 20.1: Best Practices in Rust Programming 229

1. Code Readability and Clarity..229

2. Embrace Rust's Ownership System...229

3. Error Handling 229

4. Comprehensive Testing..229

5. Documentation..229

6. Dependency Management with Cargo 229

7. Design Patterns and Architecture..230

8. Performance Optimization...230

9. Open Source Contribution and Collaboration 230

10. Lifelong Learning..230

Section 20.2: The Rust Community and Continuing Education.........................230

The Rust Community..230

Continuing Your Education 231

Section 20.3: Future-Proofing Your Rust Skills 232

   Embrace Lifelong Learning..232

   Diversify Your Skill Set..233

   Build a Strong Portfolio...233

   Stay Adaptable and Resilient 234

   Networking and Collaboration..234

Section 20.4: The Impact of Rust on Software Development 234

   1. Memory Safety and Systems Programming..234

   2. Concurrency and Parallelism...234

   3. Web Assembly (Wasm) and Browser-Based Applications 234

   4. Security and Safe Systems...235

   5. Language Design and Innovation..235

   6. Growing Ecosystem and Libraries..235

   7. Education and Learning 235

   8. Community and Collaboration 235

Section 20.5: Final Thoughts and Next Steps in Rust Programming................................236

   1. Master the Fundamentals...236

   2. Explore Specialized Domains...236

   3. Contribute to Open Source...236

   4. Stay Informed 236

   5. Experiment with Advanced Features...236

   6. Continue Learning 236

   7. Collaborate and Network..237

   8. Teach and Mentor 237

   9. Embrace Challenges..237

   10. Enjoy the Journey 237

Chapter 1: Introduction to Rust

1.1 The Origin and Philosophy of Rust

Rust, a systems programming language developed by Mozilla, has gained significant attention in recent years due to its unique design principles and capabilities. The origins of Rust can be traced back to a project within Mozilla called "Servo," which aimed to build a high-performance web browser engine. During this project, developers encountered issues with memory safety, concurrency, and control over system resources, which ultimately led to the creation of Rust.

The Birth of Rust

Rust was officially introduced to the public in 2010, with its first alpha release. It was designed as a language that provides the low-level control of systems programming while eliminating common pitfalls like null pointer dereferences, buffer overflows, and data races. This approach was a response to the challenges faced in building secure and robust software systems, especially in the context of modern web browsers.

Rust's Philosophy

At the heart of Rust's philosophy is the pursuit of three key principles:

1. **Safety**: Rust prioritizes the safety of software by preventing common programming errors at compile time. It achieves this through its ownership system and strict borrowing rules, ensuring memory safety and preventing data races.

2. **Concurrency**: Rust aims to make concurrent programming accessible and safe. It offers abstractions like threads and asynchronous programming while enforcing thread safety through the type system.

3. **Performance**: Rust does not compromise on performance. It provides control over memory layout and efficient abstractions, making it suitable for systems programming tasks where performance is critical.

Zero-Cost Abstractions

One of Rust's remarkable features is the concept of "zero-cost abstractions." This means that high-level abstractions in Rust do not come with a runtime performance penalty. Developers can use abstractions like closures, iterators, and smart pointers without sacrificing performance.

The Rust Community

Rust has a vibrant and passionate community of developers who actively contribute to its growth. The community plays a significant role in shaping the language, creating libraries (referred to as "crates" in Rust), and sharing knowledge through forums, blogs, and conferences.

Adopting Rust

Rust's unique combination of safety, concurrency, and performance has led to its adoption in various domains, including systems programming, web development, game development, and more. Its extensive ecosystem of libraries and tools makes it increasingly accessible for a wide range of projects.

In the following sections of this chapter, we will delve deeper into Rust's key features, its comparison with other programming languages, and how to set up the Rust environment for development. By the end of this chapter, you will have a solid understanding of Rust's foundations and be ready to start your journey into this exciting programming language.

1.2 Key Features of Rust

Rust stands out among programming languages due to its distinctive features, which combine safety, concurrency, and performance. In this section, we will explore some of the key features that make Rust an attractive choice for developers.

1. Memory Safety

Rust's ownership system ensures memory safety by tracking how data is used and enforcing strict rules at compile time. It eliminates common bugs such as null pointer dereferences, buffer overflows, and use-after-free errors. This feature prevents crashes and security vulnerabilities in your code.

2. Ownership and Borrowing

Rust introduces the concept of ownership, which allows only one variable to "own" a piece of data at a time. When ownership transfers, the previous owner loses access, ensuring data integrity. Borrowing allows temporary access to data without transferring ownership, with strict rules for mutable and immutable borrowing.

```
fn main() {
    let mut s = String::from("Hello, Rust!");

    // Mutable borrow
    let len = calculate_length(&mut s);

    // s is still accessible here but not mutable
    println!("Length of s: {}", len);
}

fn calculate_length(s: &mut String) -> usize {
    // Mutable borrow allows modification of data
    s.push_str(" Welcome!");
```

```
        s.len()
}
```

3. Concurrency Without Data Races

Rust makes concurrent programming safe by ensuring that data races are impossible. It employs a system of ownership, borrowing, and lifetimes to guarantee thread safety at compile time. This makes it easier to write multi-threaded code without worrying about race conditions.

```
use std::thread;

fn main() {
    let mut counter = 0;

    let thread1 = thread::spawn(|| {
        for _ in 0..5 {
            counter += 1;
        }
    });

    let thread2 = thread::spawn(|| {
        for _ in 0..5 {
            counter += 1;
        }
    });

    thread1.join().unwrap();
    thread2.join().unwrap();

    println!("Counter: {}", counter);
}
```

4. Zero-Cost Abstractions

Rust allows developers to use high-level abstractions without sacrificing performance. This concept of "zero-cost abstractions" ensures that code runs as efficiently as if the abstractions were written in a lower-level language.

```
fn main() {
    let numbers = vec![1, 2, 3, 4, 5];
    let sum: i32 = numbers.iter().sum();
    println!("Sum: {}", sum);
}
```

5. Pattern Matching

Pattern matching in Rust is a powerful feature that simplifies code by matching values against patterns and executing corresponding code blocks. It is commonly used for destructuring data structures and handling different cases elegantly.

```
fn main() {
    let number = 5;

    match number {
        1 => println!("One"),
        2 => println!("Two"),
        3 | 4 => println!("Three or Four"),
        _ => println!("Other"),
    }
}
```

6. Ownership Guarantees

Rust's ownership system guarantees certain properties in your code:

- There can be either one mutable reference or multiple immutable references to a piece of data, but not both simultaneously.
- References must always be valid during their lifetime, preventing the use of dangling pointers.
- When a variable goes out of scope, Rust automatically releases the memory associated with it, avoiding memory leaks.

These features collectively make Rust a robust and reliable language for developing a wide range of applications, from system-level software to high-performance web servers. In the following sections of this book, we will delve deeper into these features and explore how to harness Rust's capabilities effectively.

1.3 Comparison with Other Programming Languages

In this section, we will compare Rust with other popular programming languages to highlight its unique features and advantages.

1. Safety and Memory Management

Compared to languages like C and C++, Rust offers a significant advantage in terms of safety. In C and C++, developers often deal with manual memory management using pointers, which can lead to common issues like buffer overflows, null pointer dereferences, and memory leaks. Rust's ownership system, borrowing, and lifetimes provide a safer alternative. By enforcing strict rules at compile time, Rust eliminates many of these memory-related issues while maintaining low-level control.

2. Concurrency

Rust's concurrency model stands out compared to languages like Java and Python. While Java provides a high-level threading model with built-in synchronization, it can still suffer from data races and deadlocks. Python's Global Interpreter Lock (GIL) limits true parallelism in multi-threaded applications. Rust, on the other hand, guarantees thread safety at compile time, making it easier to write concurrent code without the fear of data races or locking issues.

3. Performance

Languages like Python and Ruby are known for their simplicity and ease of use, but they may suffer from slower execution speeds due to their dynamic typing and interpretation. Rust, designed with performance in mind, offers the performance of low-level languages like C and C++ while maintaining a high-level, expressive syntax. This makes Rust an excellent choice for applications that require both safety and speed.

4. Ecosystem and Libraries

Languages like JavaScript and Python have vast ecosystems and libraries available for various purposes. Rust, while still growing, has an active community that continuously develops and maintains libraries (crates) for a wide range of use cases. Additionally, Rust can easily interface with libraries written in C, providing access to a wealth of existing code.

5. Learning Curve

Languages like JavaScript and Python are often praised for their beginner-friendliness and ease of learning. Rust, while not as simple to pick up initially, offers a rewarding learning experience. Once developers grasp Rust's ownership system and borrowing, they find it easier to write reliable and safe code. Rust's compiler error messages are also known for being informative and guiding developers towards correct solutions.

6. Web Development

Languages like JavaScript and Ruby have traditionally dominated web development. However, Rust has made significant inroads in this domain with frameworks like Rocket and Actix. Rust's safety features, performance, and compatibility with WebAssembly make it a compelling choice for web development, particularly in scenarios where security and speed are critical.

7. Systems Programming

When it comes to systems programming, C and C++ have been the traditional choices. Rust, with its focus on memory safety and concurrency, is emerging as a safer alternative for system-level programming tasks. It has found applications in projects like operating system development (e.g., Redox OS), game engines, and networking.

8. Community and Support

Languages like Java and Python have extensive communities and corporate backing, which translates to robust support and resources. Rust's community may be smaller, but it is highly engaged and passionate. Rust's governance model, focused on open collaboration, ensures the language's continuous development and improvement.

In summary, Rust distinguishes itself with a unique combination of safety, concurrency, and performance. While it may not be the best fit for every project, it excels in scenarios where these qualities are crucial, such as systems programming, web development, and high-performance applications. As you explore Rust further in this book, you will gain a deeper understanding of how its features can benefit your specific development needs.

1.4 Installing and Setting Up the Rust Environment

Before you start coding in Rust, you need to set up your development environment. Rust provides a straightforward installation process for various platforms, making it accessible to a wide range of developers.

1. Installing Rust

To install Rust, visit the official Rust website at https://www.rust-lang.org/ and follow the installation instructions specific to your operating system. Rust's package manager, Cargo, is included with the installation, which simplifies project management, dependencies, and building.

2. Verifying the Installation

After installation, you can verify that Rust and Cargo are correctly installed by opening your terminal or command prompt and running the following commands:

```
rustc --version
cargo --version
```

These commands should display the installed Rust compiler and Cargo versions, confirming that the installation was successful.

3. Setting Up a Rust Project

Now that Rust is installed, you can create your first Rust project. Rust projects are managed using Cargo, which automates many tasks, such as dependency management and building.

To create a new Rust project, open your terminal and run the following command, replacing my_project with your desired project name:

```
cargo new my_project
```

This command will create a directory named my_project containing the basic structure of a Rust project, including source code files and a Cargo.toml configuration file.

4. Understanding `Cargo.toml`

The `Cargo.toml` file is essential for managing your project's dependencies and configuration. You can open this file in a text editor to modify it according to your project's requirements.

Here's an example of a minimal `Cargo.toml` file:

```
[package]
name = "my_project"
version = "0.1.0"
edition = "2018"

[dependencies]
```

In this example, you can specify the project's name, version, and Rust edition. The `[dependencies]` section is where you list any external crates (libraries) your project relies on.

5. Building and Running Your Project

Once you've set up your project and `Cargo.toml`, you can build and run it using Cargo. Navigate to your project's directory in the terminal and run the following commands:

```
cd my_project
cargo build    # Build your project
cargo run      # Run your project
```

Cargo will automatically download and build any dependencies listed in your `Cargo.toml` file. If your project is a library crate (a reusable component), you can run tests with `cargo test`.

6. Exploring Rust Documentation

Rust provides extensive documentation, both for the language itself and for libraries (crates) available on crates.io, the Rust package registry. You can access Rust's official documentation at https://doc.rust-lang.org/.

To view the documentation for a specific crate, you can use the `cargo doc` command:

```
cargo doc --open
```

This command generates and opens documentation for your project's dependencies in your web browser.

7. Integrated Development Environments (IDEs)

While Rust can be developed using a simple text editor and the command line, many developers prefer using Integrated Development Environments (IDEs) that offer features like code completion, debugging, and project management. Popular Rust-friendly IDEs include Visual Studio Code with the Rust extension, JetBrains' IntelliJ IDEA with the Rust plugin, and more.

In conclusion, setting up the Rust environment is a straightforward process, thanks to Rust's official installation packages and the power of Cargo for project management. Whether you are starting a new project or exploring existing Rust code, a well-configured Rust environment is the first step to productive and enjoyable development in this language.

1.5 Writing Your First Rust Program

Now that you have Rust installed and your environment set up, it's time to write your first Rust program. In this section, we'll walk through the process of creating a simple "Hello, World!" program in Rust.

1. Creating a New Rust Project

Before you start coding, you need to create a new Rust project. You may have already created a project in the previous section, but if not, use the following command to create a new project:

```
cargo new hello_world
```

This command creates a directory named hello_world containing the basic structure of a Rust project.

2. Editing the Main Source File

Navigate to your project's directory using your terminal or text editor. Inside the hello_world directory, you'll find a src folder with a file named main.rs. This is the main source file for your Rust program.

Open main.rs in your text editor and replace its contents with the following code:

```
fn main() {
    println!("Hello, World!");
}
```

This simple program defines a main function and uses the println! macro to print the text "Hello, World!" to the console.

3. Building and Running the Program

Now that you've written your Rust program, it's time to build and run it. In your terminal, navigate to the project's directory (hello_world) and run the following commands:

```
cd hello_world
cargo run
```

Cargo will compile your program and execute it. You should see the output "Hello, World!" displayed in your terminal.

4. Understanding the Code

Let's break down the code you wrote:

- `fn main() { ... }`: This defines the `main` function, which is the entry point of your program.
- `println!("Hello, World!");`: This line uses the `println!` macro to print the specified text to the console. The `!` indicates that it's a macro, not a regular function.

5. Expanding Your Program

Congratulations! You've successfully written and run your first Rust program. From here, you can start exploring Rust's features and capabilities. Consider expanding your program by adding more code and experimenting with Rust's syntax and concepts.

Here are some ideas to get you started:

- Declare variables and print their values.
- Explore Rust's data types, such as integers, floats, and strings.
- Create functions and call them from the `main` function.
- Experiment with control flow structures like `if` statements and loops.

As you gain more experience with Rust, you'll be able to tackle more complex projects and explore the language's unique features, such as ownership, borrowing, and pattern matching. Rust's strong type system and safety guarantees make it a powerful and reliable choice for a wide range of programming tasks. Enjoy your journey into Rust programming!

Chapter 2: Basic Concepts in Rust

2.1 Understanding Variables and Mutability

In Rust, understanding how variables work and their mutability is crucial as it is one of the fundamental concepts of the language. Unlike some other languages, Rust enforces strict rules on variable mutability to ensure memory safety and prevent common programming errors.

2.1.1 Variable Declaration and Initialization

In Rust, you declare a variable using the `let` keyword, followed by the variable name and an optional type annotation. Here's a simple example:

```
let x: i32; // Declaration without initialization
x = 5;      // Initialization
```

In the above code, x is declared without an initial value, and later it is initialized with the value 5. Rust allows you to separate variable declaration and initialization, but you must ensure that the variable is initialized before using it.

2.1.2 Mutable and Immutable Variables

In Rust, variables are immutable by default, which means once a value is assigned to a variable, you cannot change it. This behavior helps prevent unexpected changes to data. Here's an example:

```
let y = 10; // Immutable variable
y = 20;     // Error: Cannot assign to `y` because it is immutable
```

To make a variable mutable, you need to use the `mut` keyword during variable declaration:

```
let mut z = 30; // Mutable variable
z = 40;         // Valid: Changing the value of a mutable variable
```

By marking a variable as mutable, you can change its value after the initial assignment.

2.1.3 Shadowing Variables

Rust allows you to shadow a variable, which means you can declare a new variable with the same name as an existing one, effectively hiding the previous variable. Shadowing is often used to change the type or value of a variable while keeping the same name:

```
let x = 5;       // Immutable variable
let x = "hello"; // Shadowing with a different type
```

In this example, the first x is an integer, and the second x is a string. Shadowing can be useful for code readability and avoiding variable name conflicts.

2.1.4 Constants

In addition to mutable and immutable variables, Rust allows you to define constants using the const keyword. Constants must have a specified type, and their values cannot change:

```
const PI: f64 = 3.14159265359;
```

Constants are a good choice when you need a value that won't change throughout the execution of your program and when you want to ensure that the value is never accidentally modified.

2.1.5 Summary

Understanding how variables work in Rust, including their mutability, is essential for writing safe and efficient code. Rust's strict rules on mutability help prevent common programming errors and contribute to the language's reputation for memory safety. By using variables, constants, and shadowing effectively, you can write Rust code that is both expressive and reliable.

2.2 Data Types and Structures

In Rust, understanding data types is fundamental to writing effective and safe code. Rust has a strong static type system that helps prevent common programming errors and ensures memory safety. Let's explore some of the essential data types and structures in Rust.

2.2.1 Scalar Types

Rust's scalar types represent single values. The primary scalar types include:

- **Integers**: Rust supports signed and unsigned integers with various bit widths, such as i8, i16, i32, i64, u8, u16, u32, and u64. For example, i32 represents a 32-bit signed integer.

- **Floating-Point Numbers**: Rust supports both f32 and f64 for representing floating-point numbers with single and double precision, respectively.

- **Booleans**: The bool type represents boolean values true and false.

- **Characters**: Rust's char type represents a single Unicode character and is enclosed in single quotes, such as 'a' or '□' .

2.2.2 Compound Types

Compound types combine multiple values into a single type. Two primary compound types are:

- **Tuples**: Tuples allow you to group multiple values of different types into one compound type. Tuples are defined using parentheses and can have elements of different types.

```
let person: (String, i32) = ("Alice".to_string(), 30);
```

In this example, person is a tuple containing a String and an i32.

- **Arrays**: Arrays hold a fixed number of elements, and all elements must have the same data type. Arrays are defined using square brackets.

```
let numbers: [i32; 3] = [1, 2, 3];
```

Here, numbers is an array of three i32 integers.

2.2.3 Compound Data Structures

Rust allows you to define custom data structures using structs and enums. These custom types are powerful tools for modeling complex data in your programs.

- **Structs**: Structs allow you to create custom data types with named fields. They are useful for representing objects with multiple attributes.

```
struct Point {
    x: f64,
    y: f64,
}

let origin = Point { x: 0.0, y: 0.0 };
```

In this example, Point is a struct with two fields x and y.

- **Enums**: Enums define a type that can have multiple possible values. Each value is called a variant and can have associated data.

```
enum Coin {
    Penny,
    Nickel,
    Dime,
    Quarter(u32), // Variant with associated data
}

let coin = Coin::Quarter(25);
```

In this example, Coin is an enum with four variants, and the Quarter variant has an associated unsigned integer.

2.2.4 The String Type

Rust's String type is used for dynamically allocated, mutable strings. It is more flexible and versatile than string literals.

```
let mut message = String::from("Hello, ");
message.push_str("Rust!");
```

In this code, `message` is a `String` that can grow in size as you append more characters to it.

2.2.5 Ownership and Data Types

Understanding Rust's ownership system is crucial when dealing with data types. Scalar types like integers and booleans are generally stored on the stack, while compound types like `String` and custom data structures use the heap for memory allocation. Rust's ownership rules ensure memory safety and prevent issues like data races and memory leaks.

In summary, Rust's strong static type system, along with its support for compound data types like tuples, arrays, structs, and enums, provides you with powerful tools for building complex and reliable programs. When working with data types in Rust, it's important to be aware of ownership and borrowing rules to write safe and efficient code.

2.3 Control Flow in Rust

Control flow structures in Rust allow you to make decisions, loop, and execute code based on certain conditions. In this section, we will explore Rust's control flow constructs, including conditional statements and loops.

2.3.1 Conditional Statements

The if Expression

The `if` expression in Rust allows you to execute code conditionally based on a Boolean condition. Here's the basic syntax:

```
if condition {
    // Code to execute if the condition is true
} else {
    // Code to execute if the condition is false
}
```

For example:

```
let number = 5;

if number < 10 {
    println!("Number is less than 10");
} else {
    println!("Number is 10 or greater");
}
```

You can use `else if` to handle multiple conditions:

```
let number = 12;

if number < 10 {
    println!("Number is less than 10");
} else if number == 10 {
    println!("Number is exactly 10");
} else {
    println!("Number is greater than 10");
}
```

The match Expression

The `match` expression in Rust is a powerful way to handle complex conditions. It allows you to compare a value against a set of patterns and execute code based on the matched pattern. Here's a basic example:

```
let fruit = "apple";

match fruit {
    "apple" => println!("It's an apple"),
    "banana" => println!("It's a banana"),
    _ => println!("It's something else"),
}
```

The _ (underscore) is a catch-all pattern that matches any value not explicitly listed.

2.3.2 Looping Constructs

The Loop Loop

The `loop` keyword in Rust creates an infinite loop that continues until explicitly stopped using the break keyword:

```
let mut counter = 0;

loop {
    println!("Counter: {}", counter);
    counter += 1;

    if counter >= 5 {
        break; // Exit the Loop
    }
}
```

The while Loop

The `while` loop allows you to execute code repeatedly while a condition is true:

```rust
let mut counter = 0;

while counter < 5 {
    println!("Counter: {}", counter);
    counter += 1;
}
```

The for Loop

The for loop is used to iterate over collections like arrays, vectors, and ranges:

```rust
let numbers = [1, 2, 3, 4, 5];

for number in numbers.iter() {
    println!("Number: {}", number);
}
```

You can also use for with ranges:

```rust
for number in 1..6 {
    println!("Number: {}", number);
}
```

2.3.3 Flow Control in Loops

In Rust, you can control the flow of a loop using continue and break statements. continue allows you to skip the current iteration and proceed to the next, while break allows you to exit the loop prematurely.

```rust
for number in 1..=10 {
    if number % 2 == 0 {
        continue; // Skip even numbers
    }
    println!("Odd Number: {}", number);

    if number == 7 {
        break; // Exit the loop when the number is 7
    }
}
```

2.3.4 The return Statement

In Rust, you can use the return statement to exit from a function and optionally return a value:

```rust
fn add(a: i32, b: i32) -> i32 {
    let result = a + b;
    return result; // Return the result
}

fn main() {
```

```
    let sum = add(3, 5);
    println!("Sum: {}", sum);
}
```

The return statement is used to specify the value to be returned from the function.

In summary, Rust provides a variety of control flow constructs, including conditional statements (if, else, and match) and looping constructs (loop, while, and for). Understanding and using these constructs effectively are essential for writing flexible and efficient Rust programs.

2.4 Functions and Modular Programming

Functions are a fundamental part of modular programming in Rust. They allow you to break your code into smaller, reusable pieces and improve code organization and maintainability. In this section, we'll explore how to define, call, and use functions in Rust.

2.4.1 Function Definitions

You can define functions in Rust using the fn keyword. Here's the basic syntax of a function:

```
fn function_name(parameter1: Type1, parameter2: Type2) -> ReturnType {
    // Function body
    // ...
    // Optionally, return a value using the `return` keyword
    // return result;
}
```

- function_name: This is the name of the function.
- parameter1, parameter2, etc.: These are the function's parameters, each with its data type.
- ReturnType: This specifies the type of value that the function returns.

Here's an example of a simple function:

```
fn greet(name: &str) {
    println!("Hello, {}!", name);
}
```

In this example, greet is a function that takes a string slice (&str) as a parameter and prints a greeting message.

2.4.2 Calling Functions

To call a function in Rust, you simply use its name and provide the required arguments in the same order as the parameter list:

37

```rust
fn main() {
    greet("Alice");
    greet("Bob");
}
```

This code calls the greet function twice with different names, resulting in two separate greetings being printed.

2.4.3 Function Parameters and Arguments

Rust supports two types of function parameters: owned and borrowed. Owned parameters indicate that the function takes ownership of the argument, while borrowed parameters mean the function borrows a reference to the argument.

- Owned Parameters:

```rust
fn take_ownership(s: String) {
    println!("Received: {}", s);
}

fn main() {
    let s = String::from("Rust");
    take_ownership(s); // Ownership transferred to the function
    // println!("String: {}", s); // Error: s is no longer valid here
}
```

In this example, the take_ownership function takes ownership of the String, and the value of s is moved into the function. After the function call, s is no longer valid.

- Borrowed Parameters:

```rust
fn borrow_value(s: &str) {
    println!("Received: {}", s);
}

fn main() {
    let s = "Rust";
    borrow_value(s); // Borrowing a reference to s
    println!("String: {}", s); // s is still valid here
}
```

Here, the borrow_value function borrows a reference to the string slice s, and the original s variable remains valid after the function call.

2.4.4 Function Return Values

Functions in Rust can return values using the return keyword. The return type of a function is specified after an arrow ->. Here's an example of a function that returns a value:

```rust
fn add(a: i32, b: i32) -> i32 {
    a + b
```

```rust
}

fn main() {
    let result = add(3, 5);
    println!("Sum: {}", result);
}
```

In this example, the add function takes two integers as parameters and returns their sum.

2.4.5 Function Visibility

By default, functions in Rust have private visibility within their module. To make a function visible outside its module, you can use the pub keyword. This allows other modules to call the function.

```rust
mod my_module {
    pub fn public_function() {
        println!("This function is public");
    }

    fn private_function() {
        println!("This function is private");
    }
}

fn main() {
    my_module::public_function(); // Accessing a public function
    // my_module::private_function(); // Error: Cannot access a private funct
ion
}
```

In this example, public_function is accessible from outside the module, while private_function is not.

2.4.6 Function Overloading

Rust does not support traditional function overloading based on the number or types of arguments. However, Rust allows you to define multiple functions with the same name as long as their parameter lists differ in some way, such as the number or types of parameters. This is called shadowing:

```rust
fn greet(name: &str) {
    println!("Hello, {}!", name);
}

fn greet(name: &str, age: i32) {
    println!("Hello, {}! You are {} years old.", name, age);
}

fn main() {
```

39

```
    greet("Alice"); // Calls the first function
    greet("Bob", 30); // Calls the second function
}
```

In this example, there are two greet functions with different parameter lists, and Rust determines which one to call based on the arguments provided.

2.4.7 Summary

Functions are a fundamental building block of Rust programs, allowing you to modularize your code and make it more readable and maintainable. Understanding how to define, call, and use functions with various parameter types and return values is essential for effective Rust programming. Additionally, visibility modifiers like pub control the accessibility of functions, enabling you to manage the visibility of your code's components within and outside modules.

2.5 Error Handling Basics

Error handling is a critical aspect of writing reliable and robust software. In Rust, error handling is based on the concept of "Result" and "Option" enums, along with the use of the match expression. This section will explore the basics of error handling in Rust.

2.5.1 The Result Enum

In Rust, the Result enum is commonly used for error handling. It has two variants: Ok and Err. Ok represents a successful result, while Err represents an error. The Result enum is often used to return results from functions that may fail.

```
fn divide(x: f64, y: f64) -> Result<f64, &'static str> {
    if y == 0.0 {
        return Err("Division by zero");
    }

    Ok(x / y)
}
```

In this example, the divide function returns a Result<f64, &'static str>, where Ok holds the result of the division, and Err holds an error message if the division by zero occurs.

2.5.2 Handling Errors with match

To handle errors returned by functions that use the Result enum, you can use the match expression. It allows you to pattern match on the result and handle both success and error cases explicitly.

```rust
fn main() {
    let result = divide(8.0, 2.0);

    match result {
        Ok(value) => println!("Result: {}", value),
        Err(err) => println!("Error: {}", err),
    }
}
```

In this code, we use match to handle the Result. If the result is Ok, it prints the result; otherwise, it prints the error message.

2.5.3 The Option Enum

The Option enum is similar to Result but is commonly used when a function may return either a valid value (Some) or nothing (None). It is often used for cases where failure is not necessarily an error but an expected outcome.

```rust
fn find_element(arr: &[i32], target: i32) -> Option<usize> {
    for (index, &value) in arr.iter().enumerate() {
        if value == target {
            return Some(index);
        }
    }

    None
}
```

In this example, the find_element function returns an Option<usize> that either contains the index of the target element in the array or None if the element is not found.

2.5.4 Unwrapping Results and Options

To access the value inside a Result or Option, you can use the unwrap method or the expect method to explicitly handle errors.

```rust
fn main() {
    let result = divide(8.0, 2.0);
    let quotient = result.unwrap();
    println!("Quotient: {}", quotient);

    let result = divide(8.0, 0.0);
    let quotient = result.expect("Division failed");
    println!("Quotient: {}", quotient); // This line will panic
}
```

Using unwrap or expect without proper error handling can lead to a panic if the result is an error.

2.5.5 Propagating Errors

In Rust, it's common to propagate errors up the call stack using the ? operator. When used within a function that returns a Result or Option, ? will return the error early if it occurs, simplifying error handling.

```rust
fn divide_and_square(x: f64, y: f64) -> Result<f64, &'static str> {
    let result = divide(x, y)?;
    Ok(result * result)
}
```

In this example, the divide_and_square function first calls divide. If divide returns an error, the error will be propagated and returned from divide_and_square as well.

2.5.6 Custom Error Types

While you can use Result and Option with built-in error types like &str, you can also define custom error types by implementing the std::error::Error trait. Custom error types provide more context and flexibility in handling errors.

```rust
use std::error::Error;
use std::fmt;

#[derive(Debug)]
struct MyError {
    message: String,
}

impl MyError {
    fn new(message: &str) -> MyError {
        MyError {
            message: message.to_string(),
        }
    }
}

impl Error for MyError {}

impl fmt::Display for MyError {
    fn fmt(&self, f: &mut fmt::Formatter) -> fmt::Result {
        write!(f, "Custom Error: {}", self.message)
    }
}

fn main() -> Result<(), MyError> {
    let result = divide(8.0, 0.0)?;
    Ok(())
}
```

In this example, we define a custom error type `MyError` that implements the `std::error::Error` trait, allowing us to create more informative and context-rich error messages.

2.5.7 Summary

Error handling is an essential aspect of writing reliable and robust Rust code. Rust provides the `Result` and `

Chapter 3: Advanced Data Types

3.1 Exploring Enums and Pattern Matching

Enums (short for enumerations) and pattern matching are powerful features in Rust that enable you to define custom types and efficiently handle different cases or variants. In this section, we will delve into enums and their associated concept of pattern matching.

3.1.1 Enumerations in Rust

An enum in Rust defines a type that can have multiple distinct values, each known as a variant. Enums are useful for representing situations where a value can have one of several possible states. Here's the basic syntax of defining an enum:

```
enum TrafficLight {
    Red,
    Green,
    Yellow,
}
```

In this example, we've defined an enum named TrafficLight with three variants: Red, Green, and Yellow. Each variant is treated as a separate value of the TrafficLight type.

3.1.2 Using Enums

You can create instances of an enum's variant and use them in your code. For example, you can create a variable representing a traffic light:

```
let current_light = TrafficLight::Red;
```

In this case, current_light is assigned the TrafficLight::Red variant.

3.1.3 Pattern Matching

Pattern matching is a feature in Rust that allows you to destructure and inspect values in a way that matches against patterns, making it powerful for branching and decision-making. It is often used with enums to handle different variants. Here's a basic example:

```
match current_light {
    TrafficLight::Red => println!("Stop!"),
    TrafficLight::Green => println!("Go!"),
    TrafficLight::Yellow => println!("Slow down!"),
}
```

In this match expression, we are matching current_light against the possible variants of the TrafficLight enum and executing different code blocks based on the variant.

3.1.4 Exhaustive Matching

Rust enforces exhaustive matching, meaning you must handle all possible enum variants in a match expression. If you omit a variant, the code will not compile. This ensures that you explicitly consider all cases, reducing the chance of unexpected behavior.

3.1.5 Matching with Values

You can also match enums based on associated values. Let's say we have a different enum:

```
enum Option<T> {
    Some(T),
    None,
}
```

In this case, the Option enum has two variants: Some, which can hold a value of type T, and None, which represents the absence of a value.

You can match against the associated values like this:

```
let some_number = Some(42);
let no_number: Option<i32> = None;

match some_number {
    Some(value) => println!("Got a value: {}", value),
    None => println!("No value!"),
}

match no_number {
    Some(value) => println!("Got a value: {}", value),
    None => println!("No value!"),
}
```

3.1.6 Using _ for Placeholder

Sometimes, you may not need to handle all variants explicitly. In such cases, you can use the underscore _ as a placeholder for variants you want to ignore. For example:

```
enum Direction {
    North,
    South,
    East,
    West,
}

let direction = Direction::North;

match direction {
    Direction::North => println!("Heading North"),
    _ => println!("Heading in some other direction"),
}
```

In this example, we only handle the `Direction::North` variant explicitly, while using _ for the other variants.

3.1.7 Combining Patterns

You can also combine patterns using the | operator to match multiple variants with the same code block. Here's an example:

```
enum Weather {
    Sunny,
    Cloudy,
    Rainy,
    Foggy,
}

let forecast = Weather::Rainy;

match forecast {
    Weather::Sunny | Weather::Cloudy => println!("It might be a good day."),
    Weather::Rainy | Weather::Foggy => println!("Take your umbrella."),
}
```

In this code, we use | to match either `Weather::Sunny` or `Weather::Cloudy` with the first pattern and `Weather::Rainy` or `Weather::Foggy` with the second pattern.

3.1.8 Summary

Enums and pattern matching are essential tools in Rust for modeling and handling complex data structures. Enums allow you to define custom types with distinct variants, while pattern matching helps you efficiently and exhaustively handle those variants in your code. These features contribute to Rust's safety and readability by ensuring that all possible cases are considered and handled.

3.2 Generics and Their Applications

Generics are a fundamental feature in Rust that enable you to write code that works with different data types while maintaining type safety. In this section, we will explore generics and their various applications in Rust.

3.2.1 Understanding Generics

Generics allow you to write functions, structs, enums, and traits that can work with a variety of data types. Instead of specifying a concrete data type, you define a generic type parameter that represents any data type. These type parameters are typically denoted by single uppercase letters, such as T, U, or E.

Here's a basic example of a generic function that swaps the values of two variables of any type:

```rust
fn swap<T>(a: &mut T, b: &mut T) {
    std::mem::swap(a, b);
}
```

In this code, T is a generic type parameter. This function can be used to swap values of different types, including integers, strings, or custom structs.

3.2.2 Using Generics with Functions

Generics in functions allow you to write flexible and reusable code. You can use generics to write functions that work with various data types while maintaining type safety. For example, here's a generic function that finds the largest element in a slice of any type that implements the PartialOrd trait:

```rust
fn find_largest<T: PartialOrd>(list: &[T]) -> Option<&T> {
    let mut largest = None;

    for item in list {
        match largest {
            None => largest = Some(item),
            Some(&max) if item > max => largest = Some(item),
            _ => {}
        }
    }

    largest
}
```

In this code, T is a generic type parameter, and the PartialOrd trait bounds indicate that the type T must implement the PartialOrd trait to be used with this function.

3.2.3 Using Generics with Structs

Generics can also be applied to structs, allowing you to create generic data structures. For example, you can create a generic Pair struct that can hold values of any type:

```rust
struct Pair<T, U> {
    first: T,
    second: U,
}

fn main() {
    let integer_and_string = Pair {
        first: 42,
        second: "hello",
    };
```

```
    let float_and_char = Pair {
        first: 3.14,
        second: 'a',
    };
}
```

In this code, Pair is a generic struct with two type parameters T and U. You can create instances of Pair with different data types for first and second.

3.2.4 Using Generics with Enums

Enums can also make use of generics. You can define enums that can hold values of generic types. Here's an example of a generic Result enum:

```
enum Result<T, E> {
    Ok(T),
    Err(E),
}
```

In this case, Result can hold either a successful result of type T or an error of type E. This is commonly used in error handling where T represents the expected result type, and E represents the error type.

3.2.5 Using Generics with Traits

Generics are frequently used with traits to define functions and methods that work with various data types. For example, you can define a generic trait that calculates the area of shapes:

```
trait Shape<T> {
    fn area(&self) -> T;
}

struct Circle {
    radius: f64,
}

impl Shape<f64> for Circle {
    fn area(&self) -> f64 {
        std::f64::consts::PI * self.radius * self.radius
    }
}
```

In this example, the Shape trait is generic, allowing it to calculate the area of shapes with different data types (e.g., f64 for circles, i32 for squares).

3.2.6 Limiting Generics with Trait Bounds

To ensure that generics meet specific requirements or implement certain traits, you can use trait bounds. Trait bounds specify that a generic type parameter must implement a particular trait. For example:

48

```
fn print_length<T: std::fmt::Display>(value: T) {
    println!("Length: {}", value);
}
```

In this code, T is required to implement the std::fmt::Display trait to be used with the print_length function.

3.2.7 Summary

Generics are a powerful feature in Rust that enable you to write flexible and reusable code that works with different data types while maintaining type safety. They are commonly used with functions, structs, enums, and traits to create versatile and efficient code. Generics are a key part of Rust's philosophy of providing both high-level abstractions and low-level control.

3.3 Traits and Abstract Data Types

Traits in Rust provide a way to define shared behavior across different types, similar to interfaces in other languages. They allow you to specify a set of methods that types must implement to use the trait. In this section, we'll explore traits and how they are used to define abstract data types in Rust.

3.3.1 Defining Traits

You can define a trait using the trait keyword followed by the trait's name and a set of method signatures. Here's a simple example of a Drawable trait:

```
trait Drawable {
    fn draw(&self);
}
```

In this code, we define a Drawable trait with a single method draw(&self). Any type implementing this trait must provide an implementation for the draw method.

3.3.2 Implementing Traits

To make a type implement a trait, you use the impl keyword followed by the trait name and the methods' implementations. Here's an example of implementing the Drawable trait for a Circle struct:

```
struct Circle {
    radius: f64,
}

impl Drawable for Circle {
    fn draw(&self) {
        println!("Drawing a circle with radius {}", self.radius);
```

49

```
        }
}
```

Now, instances of the `Circle` struct can be treated as `Drawable` and have a draw method.

3.3.3 Trait Bounds

Trait bounds are used to specify that a generic type parameter must implement a particular trait. For example, if you have a generic function that works with types implementing the `Drawable` trait, you can use a trait bound like this:

```
fn draw_shapes<T: Drawable>(shapes: &[T]) {
    for shape in shapes {
        shape.draw();
    }
}
```

In this code, `T: Drawable` is a trait bound indicating that `T` must implement the `Drawable` trait to be used as the parameter type for `draw_shapes`.

3.3.4 Default Implementations

In Rust, you can provide default implementations for trait methods. Types implementing the trait can choose to override these default implementations if needed. Here's an example:

```
trait Greet {
    fn greet(&self) {
        println!("Hello!");
    }
}

struct Person {
    name: String,
}

impl Greet for Person {
    fn greet(&self) {
        println!("Hello, {}!", self.name);
    }
}
```

In this code, the `Greet` trait has a default greet method that prints "Hello!" by default. The `Person` struct provides its implementation for greet, which overrides the default behavior.

3.3.5 Multiple Trait Implementations

A type can implement multiple traits, allowing it to inherit behavior from multiple sources. Here's an example of a type implementing both the `Drawable` and `Greet` traits:

```
struct Rectangle {
    width: f64,
    height: f64,
}


impl Drawable for Rectangle {
    fn draw(&self) {
        println!("Drawing a rectangle with dimensions {}x{}", self.width, sel
f.height);
    }
}


impl Greet for Rectangle {
    fn greet(&self) {
        println!("Greetings from a rectangle with dimensions {}x{}", self.wid
th, self.height);
    }
}
```

Now, instances of the Rectangle struct can be treated as both Drawable and Greet types.

3.3.6 Trait Objects

In Rust, trait objects allow you to work with values of different types that implement a specific trait. You can use trait objects to create more flexible and dynamic code. Here's an example:

```
fn main() {
    let circle = Circle { radius: 5.0 };
    let rectangle = Rectangle { width: 10.0, height: 6.0 };

    let shapes: Vec<Box<dyn Drawable>> = vec![Box::new(circle), Box::new(rect
angle)];

    for shape in shapes.iter() {
        shape.draw();
    }
}
```

In this code, we create a vector of trait objects that implement the Drawable trait. This allows us to store values of different types in the same collection and call the draw method on each of them.

3.3.7 Summary

Traits are a powerful feature in Rust for defining shared behavior across different types. They allow you to create abstract data types and specify a set of methods that types must implement to use the trait. Trait bounds enable you to ensure that generic types implement specific traits, providing compile-time safety. Default implementations and multiple trait implementations add flexibility to your code, while trait objects allow you to work with values of different types that implement a trait, enhancing code dynamism and versatility. Traits are a key component of Rust's composability and code reuse principles.

3.4 Collections in Rust

Rust provides a variety of collection types that allow you to store and manipulate data in different ways. In this section, we'll explore some of the most commonly used collections in Rust, including arrays, vectors, strings, and maps.

3.4.1 Arrays

Arrays in Rust are fixed-size, contiguous collections of elements with a uniform data type. They are defined using square brackets and have a fixed length that cannot be changed at runtime. Here's an example of an array:

```
let numbers: [i32; 5] = [1, 2, 3, 4, 5];
```

In this code, we define an array named numbers with a length of 5 and elements of type i32. Accessing elements in an array is done using indexing, like numbers[2] to access the third element.

3.4.2 Vectors

Vectors are dynamic arrays in Rust that can grow or shrink in size at runtime. They are defined using the Vec<T> type. Here's an example of a vector:

```
let mut fruits = Vec::new();
fruits.push("Apple");
fruits.push("Banana");
fruits.push("Cherry");
```

In this code, we create an empty vector fruits and use the push method to add elements to it. Vectors automatically handle resizing when needed.

3.4.3 Strings

In Rust, strings are UTF-8 encoded, resizable, and represented as the String type. You can create strings from string literals or by converting other data types. Here's an example:

```
let greeting = "Hello, Rust!"; // string literal
let name = String::from("Alice"); // creating a String from a str
```

Rust also supports various string manipulation methods, making it easy to work with strings.

3.4.4 Slices

Slices are references to a portion of a collection, like arrays or vectors, rather than the whole collection. They are denoted by a range of indices and allow you to work with a subset of the data without making a full copy. Here's an example:

```
let numbers = [1, 2, 3, 4, 5];
let slice = &numbers[1..4]; // creates a slice of numbers 2, 3, and 4
```

Slices are useful for efficient and safe data manipulation.

3.4.5 HashMaps

HashMaps are a type of collection that stores key-value pairs, providing fast and efficient lookup based on keys. They are defined using the HashMap<K, V> type, where K is the key type and V is the value type. Here's an example:

```
use std::collections::HashMap;

let mut scores = HashMap::new();
scores.insert("Alice", 95);
scores.insert("Bob", 88);
```

In this code, we create a HashMap named scores and insert key-value pairs into it.

3.4.6 Iterators

Rust collections often work seamlessly with iterators, which allow you to process elements one at a time. You can use methods like map, filter, and fold to transform and manipulate data efficiently. Here's an example using a vector and iterators:

```
let numbers = vec![1, 2, 3, 4, 5];

let squared_numbers: Vec<i32> = numbers.iter().map(|x| x * x).collect();
```

In this code, we use iterators to square each element in the numbers vector and collect the results into a new vector.

3.4.7 Summary

Rust provides a versatile set of collections for storing and manipulating data, including arrays, vectors, strings, slices, and HashMaps. These collections offer various capabilities to suit different needs, such as fixed-size arrays, dynamic vectors, resizable strings, and efficient key-value mapping. Rust's emphasis on safety and performance is reflected in the design of its collection types, ensuring that you can work with data effectively while minimizing the risk of runtime errors. Iterators are a powerful tool for processing elements in collections, allowing you to apply transformations and filters in a concise and expressive manner. Understanding these collection types is essential for working with data in Rust effectively.

3.5 Smart Pointers and Memory Safety

Smart pointers in Rust are data structures that not only store the value they point to but also provide additional metadata and capabilities. They help ensure memory safety by enforcing ownership and borrowing rules at compile time. In this section, we'll explore some of the most commonly used smart pointers in Rust.

3.5.1 The Box Smart Pointer

The Box<T> smart pointer allows you to allocate values on the heap rather than the stack. It is used when you need to have a known size at compile time and want to move data ownership to the heap. Here's an example:

```
let x = 42; // an integer on the stack
let y = Box::new(42); // an integer on the heap
```

In this code, Box::new(42) creates a box that contains the integer 42 on the heap. The ownership of the integer is now transferred to the box.

3.5.2 The Rc and Arc Smart Pointers

The Rc<T> (Reference Counted) and Arc<T> (Atomic Reference Counted) smart pointers allow you to have multiple references to the same data on the heap while enforcing memory safety. Rc is for single-threaded scenarios, while Arc is for multi-threaded scenarios. Here's an example using Rc:

```
use std::rc::Rc;

let shared_data = Rc::new(vec![1, 2, 3]);
let clone1 = Rc::clone(&shared_data);
let clone2 = Rc::clone(&shared_data);
```

In this code, Rc allows shared_data to have multiple owners (clone1 and clone2) without causing data races.

3.5.3 The RefCell Smart Pointer

The RefCell<T> smart pointer is used for interior mutability, allowing you to mutate data even when it's considered immutable by Rust's borrowing rules. It performs runtime checks for ownership and borrowing. Here's an example:

```
use std::cell::RefCell;

let data = RefCell::new(vec![1, 2, 3]);
let mut borrowed = data.borrow_mut(); // Mutable borrow
borrowed.push(4); // Mutation is allowed
```

RefCell provides dynamic borrow checking, which allows mutable borrows at runtime, but it can panic if borrowing rules are violated.

3.5.4 The Mutex and RwLock Smart Pointers

The Mutex<T> (Mutual Exclusion) and RwLock<T> (Read-Write Lock) smart pointers are used for multi-threaded scenarios where you need to synchronize access to shared data. Mutex allows one thread to access data at a time, while RwLock allows multiple threads to read data simultaneously but only one to write. Here's an example using Mutex:

```
use std::sync::Mutex;

let data = Mutex::new(42);
let mut locked_data = data.lock().unwrap(); // Lock the data for exclusive ac
cess
*locked_data += 1; // Modify the data safely
```

In this code, the lock method provides exclusive access to the data, ensuring that only one thread can modify it at a time.

3.5.5 The Drop Trait

Rust's smart pointers can also implement the Drop trait to specify custom cleanup code that runs when the smart pointer goes out of scope. This is often used for resource management, such as closing files or releasing memory. Here's a simplified example:

```
struct CustomResource {
    // Constructor and other methods...

    // Implementing the Drop trait for cleanup
    fn close_resource(&self) {
        // Cleanup code here...
    }
}

impl Drop for CustomResource {
    fn drop(&mut self) {
        self.close_resource();
    }
}
```

In this code, the Drop trait allows you to define cleanup logic in the drop method, ensuring that it runs when the CustomResource smart pointer is dropped.

3.5.6 Summary

Smart pointers in Rust play a crucial role in ensuring memory safety by enforcing ownership and borrowing rules at compile time. The Box smart pointer is used for heap allocation and transferring ownership. Rc and Arc smart pointers enable shared ownership with reference counting. RefCell provides interior mutability, Mutex and RwLock allow safe concurrent access to shared data, and the Drop trait is used for custom cleanup code. Understanding and using smart pointers appropriately is essential for writing safe and efficient Rust code, particularly in multi-threaded and resource management scenarios.

Chapter 4: Ownership and Borrowing

4.1 The Ownership Model in Rust

Rust's ownership system is one of its defining features, designed to ensure memory safety without the need for a garbage collector. In this section, we will delve into the ownership model in Rust, understanding how it works and why it's crucial for writing safe and efficient code.

4.1.1 Ownership Rules

At the heart of Rust's ownership model are three key rules:

1. Each value in Rust has a variable that is its **owner**.
2. Values can have **only one** owner at a time.
3. When the owner goes out of scope, the value is automatically **deallocated**.

Let's explore these rules in more detail.

4.1.2 Ownership and Variables

In Rust, when you bind a value to a variable, that variable becomes the **owner** of the value. Ownership means that the variable is responsible for the value's memory allocation and deallocation.

```
fn main() {
    let x = 42; // x is the owner of the integer 42
}
```

In this code, x is the owner of the integer 42. When x goes out of scope, Rust will automatically deallocate the memory used by 42.

4.1.3 Ownership Transfer

Rust enforces the rule that a value can have only one owner at a time. When you assign a value to another variable, you are **transferring ownership**.

```
fn main() {
    let x = 42; // x owns 42
    let y = x;  // ownership of 42 is transferred to y
}
```

In this code, after y receives ownership of 42, you cannot use x to access it anymore. This ensures that there are no multiple owners of a value, preventing issues like double-freeing memory.

4.1.4 Ownership and Functions

When you pass a value as an argument to a function, ownership is often transferred to the function's parameter.

```rust
fn process_data(data: Vec<i32>) {
    // data owns the vector passed to the function
    // ...
} // When data goes out of scope, the vector is deallocated

fn main() {
    let values = vec![1, 2, 3];
    process_data(values); // Ownership of values is transferred to process_data
    // Cannot use values here
}
```

In this example, ownership of the vector `values` is transferred to the `process_data` function. This ensures that `values` cannot be used after it has been passed to the function.

4.1.5 Borrowing

While ownership is strict, Rust provides a mechanism for temporary access without transferring ownership, called **borrowing**. Borrowing allows you to pass references to values without giving up ownership.

```rust
fn calculate_length(s: &String) -> usize {
    // s is a reference to a String, and ownership remains with the caller
    s.len()
}

fn main() {
    let my_string = String::from("Hello, Rust!");
    let len = calculate_length(&my_string); // Pass a reference to my_string
    // my_string can still be used here
}
```

In this code, the `calculate_length` function takes a reference to a `String`, allowing it to calculate the length without taking ownership of `my_string`.

4.1.6 Ownership and Mutability

Rust's ownership model also enforces strict rules for mutable access. You can have either one mutable reference or multiple immutable references to a value, but not both at the same time.

```rust
fn main() {
    let mut data = vec![1, 2, 3];

    let r1 = &data; // Immutable reference
    let r2 = &data; // Immutable reference
```

```
    // Cannot have a mutable reference while immutable references exist
    // Let r3 = &mut data; // Error!
}
```

In this example, r1 and r2 are immutable references, and you cannot create a mutable reference r3 while they exist. This rule prevents data races and ensures memory safety.

4.1.7 Ownership and Lifetimes

Rust uses **lifetimes** to track how long references are valid to prevent dangling references. Lifetimes are annotations that specify the scope during which a reference is valid.

```
fn longest<'a>(s1: &'a str, s2: &'a str) -> &'a str {
    if s1.len() > s2.len() {
        s1
    } else {
        s2
    }
}

fn main() {
    let string1 = String::from("hello");
    let string2 = "world";

    let result;
    {
        result = longest(string1.as_str(), string2);
    } // 'result' references valid data

    println!("The longest string is: {}", result);
} // 'result' goes out of scope, references become invalid
```

In this code, the longest function uses lifetimes to specify that the returned reference should be valid as long as the input references s1 and s2 are valid.

4.1.8 Summary

The ownership model in Rust ensures memory safety by enforcing strict rules on ownership, borrowing, and mutability. Understanding and following these rules is essential for writing safe and efficient Rust code. Ownership ensures that values are deallocated properly, preventing memory leaks and data races. Borrowing allows temporary access without transferring ownership, and lifetimes ensure that references are always valid. These concepts work together to provide strong guarantees of memory safety without the need for a garbage collector.

4.2 Borrowing and References

In Rust, borrowing and references are fundamental concepts that play a crucial role in ensuring memory safety and preventing data races. Borrowing allows you to share access to data without transferring ownership, and references are used to create borrowings. In this section, we will explore borrowing and references in depth.

4.2.1 Mutable and Immutable References

Rust allows two types of references: **mutable** and **immutable**. An immutable reference (&T) allows read-only access to the data, while a mutable reference (&mut T) allows both read and write access. These references ensure that data is either read-only or exclusively writable, preventing conflicts.

```
fn main() {
    let mut data = vec![1, 2, 3];

    let r1 = &data;      // Immutable reference
    let r2 = &data;      // Immutable reference
    let r3 = &mut data;  // Mutable reference

    // Cannot have mutable reference while immutable references exist
    // Let r4 = &mut data; // Error!
}
```

In this code, r1 and r2 are immutable references, allowing read-only access to data. r3 is a mutable reference, enabling both read and write access. However, attempting to create r4 while r1 and r2 exist would result in an error due to Rust's ownership rules.

4.2.2 Borrow Checker

Rust employs a **borrow checker** that statically analyzes code to ensure that references are used safely. The borrow checker enforces rules like:

- You cannot have a mutable reference while immutable references exist.
- References must not outlive the data they point to (lifetimes).

```
fn main() {
    let mut data = vec![1, 2, 3];
    let r1 = &data;      // Immutable reference
    let r2 = &data;      // Immutable reference

    // Attempting to modify 'data' while references exist is not allowed
    // data.push(4); // Error!
}
```

In this code, trying to modify data while r1 and r2 are in scope results in an error, preventing data races.

4.2.3 Dangling References

Rust ensures that references are always valid by preventing **dangling references**, which occur when a reference points to data that has been deallocated.

```rust
fn main() {
    let r;

    {
        let data = vec![1, 2, 3];
        r = &data; // 'data' goes out of scope, 'r' would be a dangling reference
    }

    // Accessing 'r' here would be unsafe
}
```

In this code, r would become a dangling reference when data goes out of scope, but Rust prevents this situation by not allowing such references.

4.2.4 References as Function Parameters

Passing references as function parameters is a common practice in Rust, allowing functions to work on data without taking ownership. Functions can accept either mutable or immutable references.

```rust
fn modify_vector(v: &mut Vec<i32>) {
    v.push(4); // Modifying the vector via a mutable reference
}

fn main() {
    let mut data = vec![1, 2, 3];
    modify_vector(&mut data); // Pass a mutable reference to the function
}
```

In this example, modify_vector accepts a mutable reference to Vec<i32>, allowing it to modify the vector.

4.2.5 References in Structs

Structs can contain references, allowing you to create data structures that reference other data. Structs with references must use lifetimes to specify the relationships between the references and the data they point to.

```rust
struct StringHolder<'a> {
    data: &'a str,
}

fn main() {
    let text = String::from("Hello, Rust!");
    let holder;
```

```
    {
        holder = StringHolder { data: &text };
    } // 'holder' goes out of scope, but 'text' is still valid

    println!("Data in holder: {}", holder.data);
}
```

In this code, StringHolder contains a reference to a string, and the lifetime 'a is used to indicate that the reference cannot outlive the string it points to.

4.2.6 Summary

Borrowing and references are fundamental concepts in Rust that ensure memory safety and prevent data races. By enforcing rules through the borrow checker, Rust guarantees that data is accessed safely. Mutable and immutable references allow controlled access to data, and the borrow checker prevents conflicts and dangling references. Understanding how to use references effectively is essential for writing safe and efficient Rust code.

4.3 Lifetime Annotations

In Rust, lifetime annotations are a critical tool for specifying how long references are valid and preventing dangling references. Lifetimes help the Rust compiler ensure that borrowed references are used safely. In this section, we'll delve into the concept of lifetime annotations and how they are used in Rust.

4.3.1 What Are Lifetimes?

Lifetimes are a way to describe the scope during which a reference is valid. They ensure that references do not outlive the data they point to or become dangling references. Lifetimes are often denoted by single lowercase letters, such as 'a, 'b, etc., and can be attached to references.

4.3.2 Lifetime Annotations in Function Signatures

One common use of lifetime annotations is in function signatures, where they indicate the relationships between the lifetimes of function parameters and return values.

```
fn longest<'a>(s1: &'a str, s2: &'a str) -> &'a str {
    if s1.len() > s2.len() {
        s1
    } else {
        s2
    }
}
```

In this code, the lifetime annotation 'a is used to specify that the returned reference will have the same lifetime as the input references s1 and s2. This ensures that the returned reference remains valid for at least as long as the input references.

4.3.3 Lifetime Elision

Rust provides a set of **lifetime elision rules** that automatically infer lifetimes in common patterns without the need for explicit annotations. These rules make code more concise while ensuring safety. For example, the previous function can be written without explicit lifetime annotations:

```
fn longest(s1: &str, s2: &str) -> &str {
    if s1.len() > s2.len() {
        s1
    } else {
        s2
    }
}
```

In this case, the compiler infers that the lifetime of the returned reference is tied to the lifetimes of s1 and s2 based on the input and output references.

4.3.4 Lifetime Bounds

Lifetimes can also be used to specify constraints on generic type parameters in structs, enums, and trait implementations.

```
struct Ref<'a, T: 'a> {
    data: &'a T,
}

impl<'a, T> Ref<'a, T> {
    fn new(data: &'a T) -> Self {
        Ref { data }
    }
}
```

In this example, the struct Ref has a lifetime 'a associated with its reference field data. The generic type parameter T is constrained by the 'a lifetime using T: 'a, indicating that the lifetime of T must not exceed 'a.

4.3.5 Lifetime Annotations in Structs and Enums

Structs and enums can also use lifetime annotations to specify the lifetimes of their fields. This is particularly useful when defining data structures that contain references.

```
struct StringHolder<'a> {
    data: &'a str,
}

enum RefOrStr<'a> {
```

```
    Ref(&'a str),
    Str(&'a str),
}
```

In these examples, the structs `StringHolder` and `RefOrStr` use lifetime annotations to indicate the lifetimes of their reference fields.

4.3.6 Lifetime Bounds in Traits

Lifetimes can be used in trait definitions to specify lifetime bounds for associated types and method signatures. This is often seen in traits related to borrowing and references.

```
trait StringProcessor<'a> {
    fn process(&self, input: &'a str) -> &'a str;
}
```

In this trait definition, the lifetime annotation 'a is used to specify that the process method takes an input reference with the same lifetime as the trait itself.

4.3.7 Lifetime Annotations in Function Signatures

Lifetime annotations can also be used in function signatures to specify the relationships between input and output lifetimes.

```
fn first_word(s: &str) -> &str {
    s.split_whitespace().next().unwrap_or("")
}
```

In this code, the `first_word` function takes a reference to a string and returns a reference to a substring of that string. The lifetime of the returned reference is implicitly tied to the input reference, ensuring safety.

4.3.8 Lifetime Annotations in Struct and Enum Definitions

Lifetimes can be used in struct and enum definitions to indicate the lifetimes of reference fields.

```
struct RefHolder<'a, T> {
    data: &'a T,
}

enum RefOrValue<'a, T> {
    Ref(&'a T),
    Value(T),
}
```

In these examples, the structs `RefHolder` and `RefOrValue` use lifetime annotations to specify the lifetimes of their reference fields.

4.3.9 Summary

Lifetime annotations in Rust are essential for specifying how long references are valid and preventing dangling references. They are used in function signatures, generic type bounds, trait definitions, and struct/enums to ensure that references are used safely and within the appropriate lifetimes. While Rust's lifetime elision rules can simplify code, explicit lifetime annotations are sometimes necessary to clarify relationships between references and lifetimes, particularly in complex data structures and trait implementations. Understanding and using lifetimes correctly is crucial for writing safe and idiomatic Rust code.

4.4 Understanding Memory Allocation

Understanding memory allocation is crucial in Rust, especially when dealing with ownership and borrowing. Rust's ownership model relies on precise control over memory allocation and deallocation to ensure safety. In this section, we will explore memory allocation in Rust, including how it works, common memory-related issues, and best practices.

4.4.1 Stack and Heap

In Rust, memory is divided into two main areas: the **stack** and the **heap**. The stack stores data with a known, fixed size at compile time, while the heap is used for data with a dynamically determined size at runtime. Stack memory allocation and deallocation are faster than heap operations, but stack space is limited.

Variables with a fixed size, such as integers and references, are usually stored on the stack, while data with variable sizes, like strings and vectors, are typically stored on the heap.

4.4.2 Ownership and Memory Allocation

In Rust, ownership is closely tied to memory allocation and deallocation. When a value is owned by a variable, Rust ensures that the memory used by that value is automatically deallocated when the variable goes out of scope. This automatic deallocation is a key feature that prevents memory leaks.

```
fn main() {
    let s = String::from("Hello, Rust!"); // 's' owns a heap-allocated string
} // When 's' goes out of scope, the string's memory is deallocated
```

In this code, the String s owns a heap-allocated string. When s goes out of scope, Rust automatically deallocates the memory used by the string.

4.4.3 Data Copies vs. Ownership Transfers

In Rust, copying data is an efficient operation for types that implement the Copy trait, such as integers and characters. These types are stored entirely on the stack, and copying simply duplicates the data.

```
fn main() {
    let x = 42; // 'x' owns an integer on the stack
    let y = x;  // Efficient copy, 'y' also owns an integer on the stack
}
```

In this example, x is copied to y, and both variables own their separate integers on the stack.

However, for types that do not implement the Copy trait, ownership is transferred when assigning a value to another variable.

```
fn main() {
    let s1 = String::from("Hello"); // 's1' owns a heap-allocated string
    let s2 = s1;                     // Ownership of the string is transferred
to 's2'
}
```

In this code, ownership of the string is transferred from s1 to s2, and s1 can no longer be used.

4.4.4 Clone Trait

To create a deep copy of data that implements the Clone trait, you can use the .clone() method or the clone function.

```
fn main() {
    let s1 = String::from("Hello");
    let s2 = s1.clone(); // Creates a deep copy of the string
}
```

In this code, s2 contains a deep copy of the string, so both variables own separate strings on the heap.

4.4.5 Memory Leaks

Rust's ownership model ensures that memory is always deallocated when it should be, preventing memory leaks. However, it's important to note that Rust is not immune to all forms of resource leaks, especially when dealing with external resources like files and network connections. For such cases, Rust provides tools like the std::mem::forget function and the std::rc::Rc type to manage resource lifetimes explicitly.

4.4.6 Dangling Pointers

Rust also prevents the creation of **dangling pointers**, which occur when a pointer references memory that has been deallocated.

```
fn main() {
    let r;

    {
        let data = 42;
        r = &data; // 'data' goes out of scope, creating a dangling reference
    } // 'r' would be a dangling pointer here
}
```

In this code, r would become a dangling pointer when data goes out of scope, but Rust prevents this situation.

4.4.7 Summary

Understanding memory allocation is vital when working with Rust's ownership model. Rust manages memory efficiently by automatically deallocating memory when values go out of scope. The distinction between types that implement the Copy trait and those that don't affects how ownership and memory allocation work. The Clone trait can be used to create deep copies of data. Rust's ownership model and the borrow checker work together to prevent memory leaks and dangling pointers, ensuring the safety of your programs. Properly managing memory allocation and ownership is essential for writing safe, efficient, and reliable Rust code.

4.5 Ownership in Practice: Building Robust Applications

Understanding ownership is crucial for building robust and reliable applications in Rust. In this section, we will explore some practical aspects of ownership in real-world scenarios, including memory management, error handling, and strategies for designing safe and efficient Rust code.

4.5.1 Memory Management

Rust's ownership model ensures memory safety by managing memory allocation and deallocation. By tracking ownership and lifetimes, Rust prevents common issues like null pointer dereferences, buffer overflows, and data races. However, it's essential to be mindful of memory management in practice.

When designing Rust applications, consider the following memory-related practices:

- Use ownership to manage resources: Rust's ownership model extends beyond memory management. It also helps manage other resources like files, network connections, and threads. Always follow Rust's ownership rules to prevent resource leaks.

- Leverage smart pointers: Rust provides smart pointers like Box, Rc, and Arc to manage memory and references more flexibly. Use Box for heap-allocated data with single ownership, Rc for reference counting, and Arc for atomic reference counting in multi-threaded contexts.

- Avoid unnecessary cloning: Cloning data can be expensive in terms of memory and performance. When possible, use references and borrow data to avoid unnecessary copying.

- Use lifetimes effectively: Lifetimes help ensure that references are valid throughout their usage. Properly annotate lifetimes in function signatures, structs, and enums to express the intended relationships between data and references.

4.5.2 Error Handling

Error handling is another critical aspect of building robust applications in Rust. Rust's approach to error handling is based on two main types: Result and Option. Result is used for functions that can return errors, while Option is used for functions that can return a Some value or None.

When dealing with error handling in Rust:

- Use the Result type for functions that may fail and need to return an error. Handle errors using the match or ? operator to propagate them up the call stack.

```rust
fn read_file() -> Result<String, std::io::Error> {
    // ...
}

fn main() -> Result<(), std::io::Error> {
    let content = read_file()?;
    // ...
    Ok(())
}
```

- Use Option for functions that may return None when a value is not available. You can use pattern matching or the unwrap and expect methods to handle Option values.

```rust
fn find_element<T>(list: &[T], target: T) -> Option<usize>
where
    T: PartialEq,
{
    // ...
}

fn main() {
    let list = vec![1, 2, 3, 4, 5];
    let index = find_element(&list, 3);
    match index {
        Some(i) => println!("Found at index: {}", i),
        None => println!("Not found"),
    }
}
```

68

- Consider using the ? operator for concise error propagation in functions that return `Result`. This operator simplifies error handling by automatically converting `Result` values into the appropriate error type.

```rust
fn open_file() -> Result<File, io::Error> {
    // ...
}

fn read_data() -> Result<String, io::Error> {
    let mut file = open_file()?;
    let mut content = String::new();
    file.read_to_string(&mut content)?;
    Ok(content)
}
```

4.5.3 Design Patterns and Best Practices

To build robust applications in Rust, consider following these design patterns and best practices:

- Use encapsulation: Encapsulate data and functionality within structs and enums. This promotes code organization and encapsulates ownership and lifetimes.

- Implement traits: Traits provide a way to define shared behavior across types. Use traits to write generic code that works with various types, enhancing code reuse.

- Avoid unwrap in production code: While unwrap is handy for quick prototyping and debugging, it's best to handle errors more gracefully in production code. Use unwrap_or, expect, or custom error handling instead.

- Utilize testing and documentation: Write comprehensive unit tests and documentation for your code to ensure its correctness and usability. Rust's testing framework is integrated into the language and encourages a test-driven development (TDD) approach.

- Pay attention to concurrency: When building multi-threaded applications, use Rust's concurrency primitives like `std::thread::spawn`, `std::sync::Mutex`, and `std::sync::Arc` to manage threads safely and efficiently.

- Learn from the community: Rust has an active and vibrant community that shares best practices, libraries, and tools. Explore the Rust ecosystem to find solutions and patterns that fit your project's needs.

4.5.4 Summary

Ownership is a fundamental concept in Rust that helps build robust and reliable applications. Understanding memory management, error handling, and design patterns is crucial for writing safe and efficient Rust code. By following Rust's ownership rules and best practices, you can leverage the language's unique features to create high-performance and secure applications.

Chapter 5: Concurrency in Rust

5.1 Introduction to Concurrency and Parallelism

Concurrency and parallelism are essential concepts in modern software development. They allow programs to perform multiple tasks simultaneously, improving performance and responsiveness. Rust provides robust support for concurrency and parallelism while ensuring safety and preventing common concurrency issues such as data races.

5.1.1 What is Concurrency?

Concurrency is the ability of a program to execute multiple tasks concurrently, where tasks can be threads, processes, or asynchronous operations. Concurrency allows a program to make progress on multiple tasks even when it has a single CPU core. It enhances the responsiveness of applications by allowing them to perform tasks simultaneously without waiting for one task to complete before starting another.

In Rust, concurrency is typically achieved using threads, which are lightweight units of execution. Rust's standard library provides the `std::thread` module for creating and managing threads.

5.1.2 What is Parallelism?

Parallelism takes concurrency a step further by executing tasks in parallel, often on multiple CPU cores. It allows for significant performance improvements by leveraging the full processing power of modern hardware.

Rust excels at parallelism through its support for multithreading and integration with libraries like Rayon for data parallelism. With Rust, you can write code that efficiently utilizes all available CPU cores to process data concurrently.

5.1.3 Concurrency vs. Parallelism

It's essential to distinguish between concurrency and parallelism:

- **Concurrency** focuses on managing multiple tasks, allowing them to run independently and make progress simultaneously. Concurrency can be achieved on a single CPU core, making it useful for tasks like handling I/O operations and improving program responsiveness.

- **Parallelism** involves executing multiple tasks in parallel on multiple CPU cores to achieve faster computation. It's suitable for tasks that can be divided into smaller independent subtasks, such as data processing and computations.

Rust provides tools and libraries for both concurrency and parallelism, allowing developers to choose the most appropriate approach for their applications.

5.1.4 Thread-Based Concurrency

Rust's standard library provides built-in support for creating and managing threads. You can spawn a new thread using the std::thread::spawn function, which takes a closure containing the code to be executed in the new thread.

```rust
use std::thread;

fn main() {
    // Spawning a new thread
    let handle = thread::spawn(|| {
        println!("Hello from the spawned thread!");
    });

    // Wait for the spawned thread to finish
    handle.join().unwrap();

    println!("Back in the main thread.");
}
```

In this example, a new thread is spawned to execute the closure. The join method is used to wait for the spawned thread to complete.

Rust's type system ensures that data shared between threads is safe from data races, a common issue in concurrent programming. Rust enforces ownership and borrowing rules, and you can use synchronization primitives like Mutex, RwLock, and Arc for safe concurrent access to shared data.

5.1.5 Asynchronous Programming

Asynchronous programming allows you to write concurrent code that efficiently handles I/O-bound operations without the need for creating multiple threads. Rust provides a powerful async/await syntax through the async-std and tokio libraries for writing asynchronous code.

```rust
async fn fetch_data() -> Result<String, reqwest::Error> {
    // Asynchronous HTTP request
    let response = reqwest::get("https://example.com").await?;
    let body = response.text().await?;
    Ok(body)
}
```

In this example, the async fn keyword indicates an asynchronous function, and the await keyword is used to await asynchronous operations. This allows non-blocking I/O operations and efficient use of resources.

5.1.6 Summary

Concurrency and parallelism are crucial concepts in modern software development, and Rust provides robust support for both. With Rust's thread-based concurrency and asynchronous programming capabilities, you can write efficient and safe concurrent code for various use cases. Understanding the differences between concurrency and parallelism and choosing the right approach for your application is essential for building high-performance Rust applications.

5.2 Threads and Thread Safety

In Rust, threads are a fundamental tool for achieving concurrency. They allow you to run multiple pieces of code simultaneously, potentially on different CPU cores. However, with great power comes great responsibility. Managing threads correctly is essential to prevent bugs and ensure safety in your programs. In this section, we'll explore threads in Rust and how to ensure thread safety.

5.2.1 Creating Threads

Creating threads in Rust is straightforward using the `std::thread` module. You can spawn a new thread by calling the `thread::spawn` function and passing it a closure containing the code to be executed in the new thread.

```rust
use std::thread;

fn main() {
    // Spawning a new thread
    let handle = thread::spawn(|| {
        println!("Hello from the spawned thread!");
    });

    // Wait for the spawned thread to finish
    handle.join().unwrap();

    println!("Back in the main thread.");
}
```

In this example, a new thread is created and runs the provided closure concurrently with the main thread. The `join` method is used to wait for the spawned thread to complete.

5.2.2 Thread Communication

Threads often need to communicate and share data. However, sharing data between threads can lead to issues like data races if not done correctly. Rust provides tools to handle this safely.

5.2.2.1 Ownership and Borrowing

Rust's ownership system ensures thread safety by enforcing ownership and borrowing rules. Data can be shared between threads by transferring ownership or using references.

73

```rust
use std::thread;

fn main() {
    let data = vec![1, 2, 3, 4, 5];

    // Move 'data' into the closure (transfer ownership)
    let handle = thread::spawn(move || {
        println!("Data: {:?}", data);
    });

    handle.join().unwrap();
}
```

In this example, the data vector is moved into the closure, transferring ownership to the spawned thread. This prevents data races.

5.2.2.2 Mutex and Arc

When multiple threads need concurrent access to shared data, Rust provides synchronization primitives like Mutex and Arc (atomic reference counting) to ensure thread safety.

```rust
use std::sync::{Mutex, Arc};
use std::thread;

fn main() {
    let counter = Arc::new(Mutex::new(0));

    let mut handles = vec![];

    for _ in 0..10 {
        let counter = Arc::clone(&counter);
        let handle = thread::spawn(move || {
            let mut num = counter.lock().unwrap();
            *num += 1;
        });
        handles.push(handle);
    }

    for handle in handles {
        handle.join().unwrap();
    }

    println!("Final count: {:?}", *counter.lock().unwrap());
}
```

In this example, an Arc (atomic reference counting) wraps a Mutex, allowing multiple threads to safely access and modify the shared counter variable.

5.2.3 Thread Safety and Data Races

Rust's ownership system, borrowing rules, and synchronization primitives help prevent data races, a common concurrency bug where multiple threads access shared data simultaneously, leading to unexpected behavior and crashes.

By following Rust's guidelines for thread safety, you can write concurrent programs that are free from data races and other synchronization issues.

5.2.4 Thread Safety and Send/Sync Traits

Rust uses the Send and Sync traits to determine whether types are safe to send between threads (Send) or safe to share between threads (Sync). Most types in Rust are Send and Sync by default, but you can implement these traits for your custom types when necessary.

5.2.5 Summary

Threads are a powerful tool for achieving concurrency in Rust, but they come with the responsibility of ensuring thread safety. Rust's ownership system, borrowing rules, and synchronization primitives like Mutex and Arc help you write concurrent programs that are safe from data races and other synchronization issues. Understanding how to create and manage threads while following Rust's guidelines for thread safety is essential for writing reliable concurrent code.

5.3 Rust's Concurrency Guarantees

Rust is designed to provide strong guarantees of safety and thread concurrency. Its ownership system, borrowing rules, and type system work together to prevent common concurrency issues such as data races and deadlocks. In this section, we will delve into Rust's concurrency guarantees and how they make concurrent programming in Rust both safe and efficient.

5.3.1 Ownership and Borrowing

Rust's ownership system ensures that data races are virtually impossible. Only one thread can have mutable access to data at any given time. When multiple threads need to access shared data, they can do so immutably, allowing concurrent read access without the risk of data races.

```
use std::sync::Arc;
use std::thread;

fn main() {
    let data = Arc::new(vec![1, 2, 3, 4, 5]);

    let mut handles = vec![];
```

```
    for _ in 0..10 {
        let data = Arc::clone(&data);
        let handle = thread::spawn(move || {
            let sum: i32 = data.iter().sum();
            println!("Sum: {}", sum);
        });
        handles.push(handle);
    }

    for handle in handles {
        handle.join().unwrap();
    }
}
```

In this example, multiple threads are concurrently reading the data vector without any synchronization primitives, and there are no data races because of Rust's borrowing rules.

5.3.2 Send and Sync Traits

Rust's type system enforces the Send and Sync traits to provide additional safety guarantees for concurrent programming. Types that implement the Send trait are safe to transfer between threads, ensuring that ownership can be moved across threads without data races.

Types that implement the Sync trait are safe to share between threads. This means that multiple threads can have concurrent read-only access to data of such types without causing data races.

```
use std::sync::{Arc, Mutex};
use std::thread;

fn main() {
    let counter = Arc::new(Mutex::new(0));

    let mut handles = vec![];

    for _ in 0..10 {
        let counter = Arc::clone(&counter);
        let handle = thread::spawn(move || {
            let mut num = counter.lock().unwrap();
            *num += 1;
        });
        handles.push(handle);
    }

    for handle in handles {
        handle.join().unwrap();
    }
}
```

```
    println!("Final count: {:?}", *counter.lock().unwrap());
}
```

In this example, `Arc` (atomic reference counting) ensures that the `Mutex` can be safely shared between threads. The `Mutex` enforces exclusive access to its data, making sure that only one thread can modify the counter at a time.

5.3.3 The Send Trait and Concurrency

The `Send` trait is automatically implemented for types that are deemed safe to be moved between threads. This includes most primitive types and many standard library types. However, for custom types, you may need to implement the `Send` trait explicitly when necessary.

```
struct MyType;

impl Send for MyType {}
```

Implementing the `Send` trait explicitly allows you to indicate that your custom type can be safely transferred between threads.

5.3.4 The Sync Trait and Concurrency

The `Sync` trait is automatically implemented for types that are deemed safe to be shared between threads. This includes types with immutable interior mutability, like `Mutex` and `RwLock`, as well as types that are entirely read-only.

```
struct MyImmutableType;

impl Sync for MyImmutableType {}
```

Implementing the `Sync` trait explicitly can be useful when working with custom types that are safe to share between threads but aren't recognized by Rust's automatic trait implementation.

5.3.5 Summary

Rust's concurrency guarantees, stemming from its ownership system, borrowing rules, and type system, make concurrent programming safe and efficient. By enforcing strict rules around ownership and borrowing, Rust prevents common concurrency issues such as data races. The `Send` and `Sync` traits provide additional safety by specifying which types are safe to move or share between threads. These features make Rust a robust choice for concurrent programming, allowing developers to write concurrent code with confidence in its safety and reliability.

5.4 Asynchronous Programming in Rust

Asynchronous programming is a powerful technique for writing concurrent and non-blocking code. Rust provides robust support for asynchronous programming through libraries like async-std, tokio, and the built-in async/await syntax. In this section, we will explore asynchronous programming in Rust and how it allows you to write efficient and responsive code.

5.4.1 What is Asynchronous Programming?

Asynchronous programming allows you to write code that can perform multiple tasks concurrently without blocking the execution of other tasks. It's particularly useful for I/O-bound operations, such as reading from files, making network requests, and handling user input. Instead of waiting for an operation to complete, asynchronous code can yield control back to the event loop and continue executing other tasks.

In Rust, asynchronous programming is achieved using async functions and the await keyword, which allow you to write non-blocking code that can efficiently handle asynchronous tasks.

5.4.2 Asynchronous Libraries in Rust

Rust's ecosystem provides several libraries and frameworks for asynchronous programming. Two popular ones are:

5.4.2.1 async-std

async-std is a library that provides asynchronous versions of standard Rust functions and utilities. It includes essential features for asynchronous I/O, such as asynchronous file I/O, network operations, and timers. You can use it to write asynchronous code that is compatible with Rust's standard library.

```rust
use async_std::fs::File;
use async_std::io::prelude::*;

async fn write_to_file() -> std::io::Result<()> {
    let mut file = File::create("example.txt").await?;
    file.write_all(b"Hello, Async World!").await?;
    Ok(())
}

#[async_std::main]
async fn main() -> std::io::Result<()> {
    write_to_file().await?;
    Ok(())
}
```

In this example, we use async-std to asynchronously create a file, write data to it, and handle errors asynchronously.

tokio is another popular asynchronous runtime and framework for Rust. It provides tools for building asynchronous networking, file I/O, and concurrent applications. tokio is known for its robustness and performance and is widely used in the Rust community.

```rust
use tokio::fs::File;
use tokio::io::AsyncWriteExt;

#[tokio::main]
async fn main() -> std::io::Result<()> {
    let mut file = File::create("example.txt").await?;
    file.write_all(b"Hello, Tokio World!").await?;
    Ok(())
}
```

In this example, we use tokio to asynchronously create a file, write data to it, and handle errors asynchronously.

5.4.3 Benefits of Asynchronous Programming

Asynchronous programming offers several benefits, including:

- **Improved Responsiveness:** Asynchronous code can efficiently handle tasks that involve waiting for external resources, such as I/O operations and network requests. This improves the responsiveness of applications and allows them to remain interactive.

- **Efficient Resource Utilization:** Asynchronous code can efficiently utilize system resources by allowing tasks to yield control when waiting for I/O operations to complete. This reduces resource wastage and improves scalability.

- **Concurrency:** Asynchronous code can handle multiple tasks concurrently, making it suitable for scenarios with many concurrent operations.

5.4.4 async/await Syntax

Rust's async/await syntax simplifies asynchronous code, making it more readable and maintainable. async functions return a Future, which represents a value that may not be available immediately. The await keyword is used to wait for the completion of asynchronous operations, allowing the code to continue execution when the result is ready.

```rust
async fn fetch_data() -> Result<String, reqwest::Error> {
    let response = reqwest::get("https://example.com").await?;
    let body = response.text().await?;
    Ok(body)
}
```

In this example, the fetch_data function asynchronously makes an HTTP request using reqwest, waits for the response, and returns the result.

5.4.5 Summary

Asynchronous programming in Rust is a powerful tool for writing concurrent and non-blocking code. Libraries like `async-std` and `tokio` provide essential features for asynchronous I/O and task management. Rust's `async/await` syntax simplifies asynchronous code, making it more readable and maintainable. By leveraging asynchronous programming, you can build efficient and responsive applications that handle I/O-bound operations gracefully and scale to handle concurrent tasks efficiently.

5.5 Building Concurrent Applications in Rust

Building concurrent applications in Rust is a powerful capability that allows you to create efficient and responsive software. In this section, we will explore the key concepts and techniques for building concurrent applications in Rust, leveraging the language's features for thread-based concurrency, asynchronous programming, and synchronization.

5.5.1 Identifying Concurrent Tasks

Before building a concurrent application, it's crucial to identify tasks that can be executed concurrently. These tasks can be broken down into two categories:

- **Independent Tasks:** Tasks that can run concurrently without affecting each other and don't require shared access to data. These tasks can be executed in parallel on multiple threads or as asynchronous operations.

- **Shared Tasks:** Tasks that need to access shared data and must be synchronized to prevent data races. These tasks often involve using synchronization primitives like `Mutex`, `RwLock`, or channels for communication.

5.5.2 Thread-Based Concurrency

Rust provides excellent support for thread-based concurrency using its standard library. You can create and manage threads using the `std::thread` module, as demonstrated earlier in Section 5.2.1. Thread-based concurrency is suitable for CPU-bound tasks that can benefit from parallelism.

5.5.3 Asynchronous Programming

Asynchronous programming, covered in Section 5.4, is essential for handling I/O-bound tasks efficiently. Rust's `async/await` syntax and libraries like `async-std` and `tokio` enable you to write non-blocking code that can handle multiple asynchronous operations concurrently.

5.5.4 Synchronization

When multiple threads need to access shared data, synchronization is critical to prevent data races and ensure correctness. Rust provides synchronization primitives like Mutex and RwLock for managing access to shared data safely. Mutexes ensure exclusive access to data, while RwLocks allow for multiple read accesses or exclusive write access.

```rust
use std::sync::{Mutex, Arc};
use std::thread;

fn main() {
    let data = Arc::new(Mutex::new(0));

    let mut handles = vec![];

    for _ in 0..10 {
        let data = Arc::clone(&data);
        let handle = thread::spawn(move || {
            let mut num = data.lock().unwrap();
            *num += 1;
        });
        handles.push(handle);
    }

    for handle in handles {
        handle.join().unwrap();
    }

    println!("Final count: {:?}", *data.lock().unwrap());
}
```

In this example, Arc (atomic reference counting) and Mutex are used to ensure safe access to the shared data variable across multiple threads.

5.5.5 Channels for Communication

Channels are a communication mechanism for passing data between threads. Rust's standard library provides the std::sync::mpsc module for creating multiple-producer, single-consumer channels. Channels are useful for coordinating and exchanging data between concurrent tasks.

```rust
use std::sync::mpsc;
use std::thread;

fn main() {
    let (sender, receiver) = mpsc::channel();

    for i in 0..5 {
        let sender = sender.clone();
        thread::spawn(move || {
```

```
            sender.send(i).unwrap();
    });
}

for _ in 0..5 {
    let received = receiver.recv().unwrap();
    println!("Received: {}", received);
}
}
```

In this example, multiple threads produce values and send them through the channel, while the main thread receives and prints them. Channels help ensure orderly communication between threads.

5.5.6 Choosing the Right Concurrency Model

Choosing the appropriate concurrency model depends on the nature of your application and its specific requirements. Rust provides multiple options, including thread-based concurrency, asynchronous programming, and a combination of both, depending on the tasks you need to perform concurrently.

Understanding your application's requirements and the characteristics of your tasks will guide your choice of concurrency model and synchronization mechanisms.

5.5.7 Summary

Building concurrent applications in Rust involves identifying tasks that can run concurrently, leveraging thread-based concurrency and asynchronous programming, and using synchronization mechanisms like mutexes, RwLocks, and channels to ensure safety and coordination among concurrent tasks. Rust's rich concurrency support makes it a versatile choice for developing software that takes full advantage of modern hardware and can efficiently handle both CPU-bound and I/O-bound tasks concurrently.

6.1 Advanced Error Handling Techniques

In Rust, error handling is a fundamental aspect of writing reliable and robust code. While Rust's standard error handling mechanism using Result and Option types is powerful and expressive, there are scenarios where you might need more advanced error handling techniques to handle complex error scenarios or implement custom error types. In this section, we will explore some advanced error handling techniques in Rust.

Result Combinators

Rust's `Result` type comes with several built-in methods that make error handling more convenient and expressive. These methods are often referred to as "result combinators." They allow you to perform operations on `Result` values without explicitly handling the `Ok` and `Err` cases each time.

One common result combinator is `map`, which lets you apply a function to the `Ok` variant if it exists while leaving the `Err` variant unchanged. This can be useful when you want to transform the successful result but leave errors untouched.

```rust
fn parse_and_double(s: &str) -> Result<i32, std::num::ParseIntError> {
    s.parse::<i32>().map(|num| num * 2)
}

fn main() {
    let result = parse_and_double("42");

    match result {
        Ok(value) => println!("Doubled value: {}", value),
        Err(err) => eprintln!("Error: {}", err),
    }
}
```

In this example, the `map` combinator is used to parse an integer from a string and double it if parsing succeeds. If there's an error during parsing, the error is propagated unchanged.

Another useful combinator is `and_then`, which allows you to chain multiple `Result`-producing functions together, only continuing if each step returns `Ok`. If any step returns `Err`, the error is propagated.

```rust
fn parse_positive_even(s: &str) -> Result<i32, String> {
    s.parse::<i32>()
        .and_then(|num| {
            if num % 2 == 0 && num > 0 {
                Ok(num)
            } else {
                Err("Not a positive even number".to_string())
            }
        })
}

fn main() {
    let result = parse_positive_even("42");

    match result {
        Ok(value) => println!("Valid positive even number: {}", value),
        Err(err) => eprintln!("Error: {}", err),
    }
}
```

Here, the and_then combinator is used to validate that the parsed integer is both positive and even. If the conditions are met, the result is Ok; otherwise, an error message is returned.

Custom Error Types

While Rust's built-in error types like std::io::Error or std::num::ParseIntError cover many common cases, you may encounter situations where you need to define your custom error types to represent specific error conditions in your application.

To create a custom error type, you define an enum that implements the std::error::Error trait. This allows you to define your error variants and provide custom behavior for error messages.

```rust
use std::error::Error;
use std::fmt;

#[derive(Debug)]
enum MyError {
    InvalidInput,
    NotFound,
}

impl fmt::Display for MyError {
    fn fmt(&self, f: &mut fmt::Formatter<'_>) -> fmt::Result {
        match self {
            MyError::InvalidInput => write!(f, "Invalid input provided"),
            MyError::NotFound => write!(f, "Requested item not found"),
        }
    }
}

fn main() -> Result<(), Box<dyn Error>> {
    // Example of using the custom error type
    let input = "invalid";
    let result: Result<i32, MyError> = input.parse()?;

    match result {
        Ok(_) => Ok(()),
        Err(err) => {
            eprintln!("Error: {}", err);
            Err(Box::new(err))
        }
    }
}
```

In this example, the MyError enum represents custom error variants, and the Display trait is implemented to provide human-readable error messages. The main function demonstrates how to use this custom error type with the ? operator for error propagation.

Recoverable vs. Unrecoverable Errors

In Rust, errors are categorized into two main types: recoverable and unrecoverable errors. Recoverable errors are typically represented using the Result type and signify errors that your program can handle and recover from. Unrecoverable errors are represented using the panic! macro and indicate severe errors that should cause the program to terminate.

It's essential to distinguish between these two types of errors and use them appropriately in your code. Recoverable errors should be handled gracefully, while unrecoverable errors should be reserved for situations where continuing the program execution would lead to undefined or unsafe behavior.

```rust
fn main() {
    let divisor = 0;
    let result = if divisor != 0 {
        42 / divisor
    } else {
        panic!("Division by zero");
    };
    println!("Result: {}", result);
}
```

In this example, attempting to divide by zero is an unrecoverable error, so it's handled using the panic! macro, which terminates the program with an error message.

Summary

Advanced error handling in Rust involves using result combinators like map and and_then for convenient error handling, defining

---

6.2 Using Rust's Debugging Tools

Debugging is an essential skill for any programmer, and Rust provides a set of powerful tools to help you identify and fix issues in your code. In this section, we will explore some of the debugging tools and techniques available in Rust.

Printing Debug Information

The most basic way to debug your Rust code is by using the println! macro to print debug information to the console. You can insert println! statements at various points in your code to inspect variables, values, and execution flow.

```rust
fn main() {
    let x = 42;
    let y = 12;

    println!("Debugging information:");
```

```rust
    println!("x: {}", x);
    println!("y: {}", y);

    let result = add(x, y);
    println!("Result: {}", result);
}

fn add(a: i32, b: i32) -> i32 {
    a + b
}
```

In this example, we use println! to print the values of x and y before calling the add function. This helps us inspect the values and debug potential issues.

Using the dbg! Macro

Rust introduced the dbg! macro, which is a convenient way to print and inspect values during debugging. It's particularly useful when you want to avoid adding and removing println! statements repeatedly.

```rust
fn main() {
    let x = 42;
    let y = 12;

    let result = add(x, y);

    dbg!(x, y, result);
}

fn add(a: i32, b: i32) -> i32 {
    a + b
}
```

When you use dbg!, it will print the variable names and their values. This can be a more concise way to inspect variables during debugging.

Debugging with eprintln!

While println! and dbg! are useful for debugging during development, Rust provides eprintln! for printing error messages to the standard error stream. This can be especially helpful when debugging applications in production or situations where you want to separate debugging output from regular program output.

```rust
fn main() {
    let x = 42;
    let y = 12;

    let result = add(x, y);

    eprintln!("Debugging information:");
```

```rust
    eprintln!("x: {}", x);
    eprintln!("y: {}", y);
    eprintln!("Result: {}", result);
}

fn add(a: i32, b: i32) -> i32 {
    a + b
}
```

In this example, we use eprintln! to print debugging information to the standard error stream, which is separate from the standard output. This helps keep debugging output isolated and easily accessible when needed.

Using the RUST_LOG Environment Variable

Rust includes a built-in logging framework that allows you to control the verbosity of log messages at runtime. You can use the log crate in your project to create and configure loggers. By setting the RUST_LOG environment variable, you can control which log messages are displayed and at what log levels.

```rust
use log::{info, error};

fn main() {
    // Set the RUST_LOG environment variable to control log levels.
    std::env::set_var("RUST_LOG", "my_app=info");

    // Initialize the logger.
    env_logger::init();

    info!("This is an informational message.");
    error!("This is an error message.");
}
```

In this example, we set the RUST_LOG environment variable to display log messages at the info level for a logger named "my_app." This allows you to control the level of detail in your application's logs without modifying the code.

Using a Debugger

In addition to print-based debugging, Rust also supports using debuggers like GDB or LLDB for more advanced debugging tasks. You can use these debuggers to set breakpoints, inspect variables, and step through your code line by line.

To use a debugger, you'll need to compile your Rust code with debugging information included. You can do this by adding the --debug flag when building your project with Cargo:

```
cargo build --debug
```

Once your project is built with debugging information, you can use GDB or LLDB to debug it.

Summary

Debugging is a crucial skill for writing robust Rust code. Rust provides several tools and techniques, including println!, dbg!, eprintln!, and the RUST_LOG environment variable, to help you identify and fix issues in your code. Additionally, using a debugger like GDB or LLDB can be invaluable for more complex debugging scenarios.

6.3 Writing Testable Code

Writing testable code is a fundamental practice in software development, and Rust provides excellent support for writing unit tests and integration tests. In this section, we will explore how to write testable code in Rust and use the built-in testing framework.

Writing Unit Tests

Rust's unit testing framework is integrated into the language and is simple to use. To write unit tests for your code, you can create a module named tests in your source file and annotate your test functions with the #[cfg(test)] attribute.

Here's an example of writing a unit test for a simple function:

```rust
// src/lib.rs or src/main.rs

pub fn add(a: i32, b: i32) -> i32 {
    a + b
}

#[cfg(test)]
mod tests {
    use super::add;

    #[test]
    fn test_add() {
        assert_eq!(add(2, 3), 5);
        assert_eq!(add(-1, 1), 0);
        assert_eq!(add(0, 0), 0);
    }
}
```

In this example, we have a function add that performs addition. The unit test module tests contains a test function test_add that uses the assert_eq! macro to check the expected results of the add function for different inputs.

To run the tests, you can use the `cargo test` command:

```
cargo test
```

As your project grows, you might have multiple modules and files containing code that needs testing. Rust provides a flexible way to organize tests in separate modules and files.

For example, you can create a separate file named `my_module.rs` and write tests for functions in that module as follows:

```rust
// src/my_module.rs

pub fn multiply(a: i32, b: i32) -> i32 {
    a * b
}

// tests/my_module_tests.rs

#[cfg(test)]
mod tests {
    use my_module::multiply;

    #[test]
    fn test_multiply() {
        assert_eq!(multiply(2, 3), 6);
        assert_eq!(multiply(-1, 1), -1);
        assert_eq!(multiply(0, 5), 0);
    }
}
```

To run tests from separate files or modules, you can use the following command:

```
cargo test --test my_module_tests
```

Writing Integration Tests

In addition to unit tests, Rust also allows you to write integration tests that test the interactions between different parts of your code or test the behavior of your application as a whole.

Integration tests are placed in a separate `tests` directory in your project, and each test file is treated as its own crate. This means integration tests have access to your library's public API just like any other external code.

Here's an example of writing an integration test for a library crate:

```rust
// lib.rs (or your library's entry point)

pub fn greet(name: &str) -> String {
```

```rust
    format!("Hello, {}!", name)
}

// tests/integration_test.rs

extern crate my_library;

use my_library::greet;

#[test]
fn test_greet() {
    assert_eq!(greet("Alice"), "Hello, Alice!");
    assert_eq!(greet("Bob"), "Hello, Bob!");
}
```

To run integration tests, you can use the following command:

```
cargo test --test integration_test
```

Test Attributes and Features

Rust provides various attributes and features to control the behavior of tests. For example, you can use the #[ignore] attribute to skip specific tests, the #[should_panic] attribute to mark tests that should panic, and the #[cfg] attribute to conditionally compile tests based on features or configurations.

```rust
#[test]
#[ignore]
fn ignored_test() {
    // This test will be ignored when running `cargo test`.
    // Useful for temporarily disabling tests.
}

#[test]
#[should_panic]
fn test_panic() {
    // This test is expected to panic during execution.
    panic!("This test should panic!");
}

#[cfg(test)]
mod conditional_tests {
    #[cfg(feature = "feature_x")]
    #[test]
    fn test_feature_x() {
        // This test is only compiled and run if the "feature_x" feature is enabled.
    }

    #[cfg(not(feature = "feature_x"))]
```

```rust
    #[test]
    fn test_without_feature_x() {
        // This test is only compiled and run if the "feature_x" feature is d
isabled.
    }
}
```

Summary

Writing testable code is essential for ensuring the correctness and reliability of your Rust applications. Rust's built-in testing framework provides a straightforward way to write unit tests and integration tests, allowing you to catch bugs early in the development process and maintain code quality as your project grows. By organizing your tests effectively and using attributes and features, you can create a robust testing strategy for your Rust codebase.

6.4 Benchmarking and Performance Analysis

Efficient code is crucial for achieving optimal performance in Rust applications. Rust provides built-in support for benchmarking and performance analysis to help you identify bottlenecks and optimize your code. In this section, we will explore how to benchmark Rust code using the bencher crate and perform basic performance analysis.

Benchmarking with bencher

The bencher crate is a commonly used library for benchmarking Rust code. To use it, you need to add it as a dependency in your Cargo.toml file:

```toml
[dev-dependencies]
bencher = "0.5"
```

Here's an example of how to write a simple benchmark test using the bencher crate:

```rust
#![feature(test)]

extern crate test;

use test::Bencher;

fn add(a: i32, b: i32) -> i32 {
    a + b
}

#[bench]
fn bench_add(b: &mut Bencher) {
    b.iter(|| add(2, 3));
}
```

In this example, we define a benchmark function bench_add and annotate it with #[bench].
Inside the benchmark function, we use the b.iter(|| ...) method to specify the code to
be benchmarked. In this case, we're measuring the performance of the add function with
inputs 2 and 3.

To run the benchmarks, use the following command:

```
cargo bench
```

After running benchmarks, you'll get detailed performance measurements, including the
number of iterations, the time taken per iteration, and the throughput in iterations per
second.

```
test bench_add ... bench:        34 ns/iter (+/- 2)
```

The result above indicates that the add function takes approximately 34 nanoseconds per
iteration. The "+/- 2" represents the measurement's standard deviation, indicating the
benchmark's variability.

You can use these results to compare the performance of different implementations and
identify areas for optimization in your code.

Profiling with cargo flamegraph

The cargo flamegraph tool allows you to generate flamegraphs, which are visual
representations of CPU usage over time. Flamegraphs help pinpoint which parts of your
code consume the most CPU resources.

To use cargo flamegraph, you need to install it:

```
cargo install flamegraph
```

Once installed, you can profile your Rust application with the following command:

```
cargo flamegraph
```

This generates a flamegraph visualization in SVG format, which you can open in a web
browser to analyze CPU usage.

cargo fmt and Code Formatting

Consistent code formatting is essential for code readability and maintainability. Rust
provides the rustfmt tool, which automatically formats your code according to the Rust
style guidelines.

To format your code using rustfmt, run the following command:

```
cargo fmt
```

`rustfmt` will reformat your code according to the conventions specified in the `.rustfmt.toml` configuration file. This ensures that your code adheres to the community's coding standards and improves code consistency in your project.

Profiling with `cargo-profiler`

The `cargo-profiler` tool provides a convenient way to profile your Rust code and analyze its performance. It supports various profiling methods, including CPU profiling with `perf` and memory profiling with `heaptrack`.

To use `cargo-profiler`, you first need to install it:

```
cargo install cargo-profiler
```

Then, you can use it to profile your code:

```
cargo profiler [options] -- <your-command>
```

For example, to profile a program using CPU profiling:

```
cargo profiler perf record -- my_program
```

This records the CPU usage of your program and generates a report that you can inspect to identify performance bottlenecks.

Summary

Optimizing the performance of your Rust code is essential, especially for resource-intensive applications. Rust provides tools like the `bencher` crate for benchmarking, `cargo flamegraph` for profiling CPU usage, and `cargo-profiler` for more advanced profiling and analysis. By utilizing these tools and following code formatting best practices with `rustfmt`, you can ensure that your Rust applications are both efficient and maintainable.

6.5 Common Rust Programming Mistakes and Solutions

While Rust promotes safe and reliable code, developers, especially newcomers, may encounter common programming mistakes. In this section, we'll explore some of these pitfalls and provide solutions to help you write better Rust code.

1. Ownership and Borrowing Errors

Rust's ownership system can lead to errors related to ownership, borrowing, and lifetimes. Common issues include:

- **Borrowing Mutably and Immutably Simultaneously:** You cannot have both mutable and immutable references to the same data simultaneously. This can lead to compilation errors.

```
let mut data = vec![1, 2, 3];
let r1 = &data;        // Immutable borrow
let r2 = &mut data;    // Mutable borrow (error)
```

Solution: Ensure that you don't have conflicting references to the same data at the same time. Refactor your code to avoid this situation.

- **Dangling References:** References that point to data that no longer exists can cause runtime errors.

```
fn get_reference() -> &i32 {
    let value = 42;
    &value // Returning a reference to a local variable (error)
}
```

Solution: Make sure references have valid lifetimes and don't outlive the data they reference. Use owned values or Rc/Arc for shared ownership when needed.

- **Lifetimes and Function Signatures:** Incorrect lifetime annotations or missing lifetimes in function signatures can lead to borrow checker errors.

```
fn longest<'a>(s1: &str, s2: &str) -> &'a str {
    if s1.len() > s2.len() {
        s1
    } else {
        s2
    }
}
```

Solution: Use lifetime annotations correctly to specify relationships between data and their references. Ensure lifetimes match the intended scope.

2. Null Pointer Errors

Rust doesn't have null pointers, but it has an Option enum for handling optional values. Misusing Option or dereferencing a None value can lead to runtime errors.

```
fn main() {
    let value: Option<i32> = None;
    println!("Value: {}", value.unwrap()); // Panics at runtime
}
```

Solution: Check and handle Option values using methods like match, if let, or the unwrap_or family of methods to provide default values.

3. Uninitialized Variables

Rust doesn't allow the use of uninitialized variables. Attempting to use a variable before initializing it will result in a compilation error.

```
fn main() {
    let x: i32;
    println!("Value: {}", x); // Use of uninitialized variable (error)
}
```

Solution: Initialize variables before using them, either through assignment or function calls.

4. Missing Result Handling

Ignoring errors returned by Result can lead to unexpected runtime failures. Common mistakes include not using the ? operator or ignoring error values.

```
use std::fs::File;

fn main() {
    let file = File::open("nonexistent.txt"); // May return Result
    let _ = file.unwrap(); // Ignoring the error (bad practice)
}
```

Solution: Handle errors returned by Result using pattern matching or the ? operator for concise error propagation.

5. Incorrect Use of unwrap

Excessive use of unwrap can lead to panics at runtime, making code unreliable. It should be used with caution and for situations where a panic indicates an unrecoverable error.

```
fn main() {
    let data: Option<i32> = None;
    let value = data.unwrap(); // Panics if `data` is `None`
}
```

Solution: Prefer using match, if let, or other error-handling techniques to handle optional or error-prone values instead of unwrap.

6. Mutable Variables When Immutability Is Sufficient

Using mutable variables unnecessarily can lead to complex code and potential bugs. In Rust, prefer immutability when you don't need to mutate data.

```
fn main() {
    let mut counter = 0;
    for _ in 0..10 {
        counter += 1; // Mutable variable for counting (could be immutable)
    }
}
```

Solution: Use let for immutable variables unless you have a valid reason to make them mutable.

7. Inefficient String Manipulation

Inefficient string manipulation, such as repeatedly concatenating strings with +, can lead to performance issues. Rust provides more efficient ways to work with strings, like String::push_str or format!.

```
fn main() {
    let mut result = String::new();
    for word in vec!["Hello", "World", "!"] {
        result += word; // Inefficient string concatenation
    }
}
```

Solution: Use more efficient string manipulation methods to avoid unnecessary allocations and copying.

8. Unnecessary Cloning

Cloning data unnecessarily can lead to performance problems. Rust provides borrowing and references for efficient data sharing.

```
fn main() {
    let data = vec![1, 2, 3];
    let _copy = data.clone(); // Unnecessary cloning
}
```

Solution: Use references (&) or borrow data when you need to share it without modifying it.

9. Missing Documentation and Comments

Lack of documentation and comments can make code hard to understand and maintain. It's essential to document your code and provide clear explanations for complex logic.

Solution: Use Rust's built-in documentation features (/// for documentation comments) and add comments to clarify your code's purpose and behavior.

10. Ignoring Warnings

Chapter 7: Rust's Ecosystem and Tooling

7.1 Understanding Cargo and Crates

Cargo is Rust's package manager and build tool, and it plays a pivotal role in managing dependencies, building projects, and handling various tasks in the Rust ecosystem. In this section, we'll delve into the fundamentals of Cargo and explore the concept of crates in Rust.

What is Cargo?

Cargo is a command-line tool that simplifies many aspects of Rust development, including:

- **Dependency Management:** Cargo allows you to declare project dependencies in a file called `Cargo.toml`. It fetches and manages these dependencies automatically, ensuring your project always has the required libraries.

- **Building and Compilation:** Cargo handles building and compiling Rust code. You can use it to compile your project, run tests, and generate documentation.

- **Package Publishing:** Cargo makes it easy to publish your Rust code as a crate on crates.io, the official Rust package registry.

Crates in Rust

In Rust, a crate is a collection of modules that provides functionality. A crate can be a library crate or an application crate. Here's what you need to know:

- **Library Crate:** A library crate contains reusable code that can be used by other projects. It doesn't have a `main` function and is meant to be a building block for other Rust programs. Libraries are shared with other Rust projects by specifying them as dependencies in the `Cargo.toml` file.

- **Application Crate:** An application crate has a `main` function and is meant to be executed. It typically uses one or more library crates to accomplish its tasks. When you create a new Rust project using `cargo new`, it generates an application crate by default.

Creating a New Rust Project

To create a new Rust project, you can use the `cargo new` command followed by the project name. For example:

```
cargo new my_project
```

This command will generate a new directory called my_project containing the necessary files and folder structure for a Rust project. Inside the project directory, you'll find:

- Cargo.toml: This is the project's configuration file. It contains metadata about the project and its dependencies.

- src directory: This directory holds the Rust source code for your project. The main.rs file inside src is the entry point for your application crate.

Managing Dependencies with Cargo.toml

The Cargo.toml file is crucial for managing dependencies in your Rust project. It specifies the project's name, version, authors, and dependencies. Here's a basic example:

```
[package]
name = "my_project"
version = "0.1.0"
authors = ["Your Name <your@email.com>"]

[dependencies]
```

In the [dependencies] section, you can specify the crates your project depends on. For example, to add the popular rand crate as a dependency, you can modify Cargo.toml as follows:

```
[dependencies]
rand = "0.8.5"
```

When you run cargo build, Cargo will download and build the rand crate and its dependencies, making them available for your project to use.

Building and Running a Rust Project

Once you've created your Rust project and specified its dependencies in Cargo.toml, you can build and run it using Cargo's commands:

- cargo build: This command compiles your project.

- cargo run: This command builds and runs your project.

- cargo test: This command runs tests in your project.

- cargo doc: This command generates documentation for your project's code.

Cargo also offers many other features and commands for various tasks. You can explore them further as you progress in your Rust development journey.

Publishing Your Crate

If you've developed a library crate and want to share it with the Rust community, you can publish it on crates.io. Publishing a crate involves creating an account on crates.io and using Cargo to manage the publishing process.

Here's a high-level overview of the publishing process:

1. Create an account on crates.io.

2. Add your crate to your `Cargo.toml` as a dependency in another project to ensure it's working as expected.

3. Use `cargo login` to authenticate with your crates.io account.

4. Use `cargo publish` to publish your crate to crates.io.

5. Once published, others can easily use your crate by adding it as a dependency in their projects.

Remember to follow best practices for versioning and documentation when publishing your crate to make it accessible and useful to the Rust community.

Conclusion

Understanding Cargo and how it manages crates is essential for Rust development. It simplifies the process of managing dependencies, building projects, and publishing crates, making Rust development more efficient and collaborative. As you delve deeper into Rust, you'll find Cargo to be an indispensable tool in your development workflow.

In the next sections of this book, we'll explore various aspects of Rust's ecosystem and tooling, including managing dependencies, working with documentation, integrating Rust with other languages, and publishing your own crates.

7.2 Managing Dependencies

Managing dependencies is a crucial aspect of software development, and Rust's package manager, Cargo, excels in this regard. In this section, we'll delve into the world of dependency management in Rust, including how to add, update, and manage dependencies for your Rust projects using Cargo.

Adding Dependencies

To add dependencies to your Rust project, you need to edit the `Cargo.toml` file. This file is located at the root of your project and is used to specify project metadata and dependencies. To add a new dependency, you can use the [dependencies] section of `Cargo.toml`.

Let's say you want to add the popular serde crate, which is used for serialization and deserialization in Rust, as a dependency. You can do this by adding the following line to your `Cargo.toml` file:

```
[dependencies]
serde = "1.0"
```

In this example, we're specifying that we want to use version 1.0 of the serde crate. When you run cargo build, Cargo will fetch and build the serde crate and make it available for your project.

Specifying Version Constraints

It's common to specify version constraints for dependencies to ensure that your project can work with a range of compatible versions. In Rust, you can use various operators to specify version constraints in your Cargo.toml.

- "=1.0": Exact version 1.0.
- ">=1.0": Any version greater than or equal to 1.0.
- "<=1.0": Any version less than or equal to 1.0.
- "^1.0": Compatible with version 1.0 (allows updates for the same minor version).
- "~1.0": Compatible with version 1.0 (allows updates for the same patch version).

Here's an example of specifying version constraints for multiple dependencies:

```
[dependencies]
serde = "1.0"
tokio = "^1.5"
reqwest = "0.11"
```

Updating Dependencies

Over time, new versions of dependencies may become available with bug fixes, improvements, or new features. To update your project's dependencies to their latest compatible versions, you can use the cargo update command. This command will update the Cargo.lock file to reflect the latest versions while respecting the version constraints specified in your Cargo.toml.

```
cargo update
```

After running cargo update, you can review the changes in the Cargo.lock file to see the updated versions of your dependencies.

Locking Dependencies with Cargo.lock

Cargo generates a file called Cargo.lock to ensure that your project consistently uses the same versions of dependencies. The Cargo.lock file records the exact versions of each dependency used when you last built your project.

You should **not** edit the Cargo.lock file manually. Instead, manage dependencies through the Cargo.toml file and let Cargo update the Cargo.lock file as needed.

Building and Managing Dependencies

Once you've added or updated dependencies in your Cargo.toml, you can build your project as usual with the cargo build command. Cargo will ensure that all dependencies are downloaded and built before compiling your project.

```
cargo build
```

Cargo also provides additional commands for managing dependencies, such as:

- `cargo tree`: Displays a tree-like structure of your project's dependencies.
- `cargo doc`: Generates documentation for your project and its dependencies.
- `cargo search`: Searches for crates on crates.io.

Conclusion

Managing dependencies in Rust using Cargo is straightforward and efficient. You can specify your project's dependencies, including version constraints, and Cargo will take care of fetching, building, and managing them. Regularly updating your dependencies is essential to benefit from bug fixes and improvements while maintaining compatibility. Additionally, the `Cargo.lock` file ensures that your project consistently uses the same dependency versions, providing stability in your development workflow.

7.3 Rust Documentation and Community Resources

Rust offers a robust ecosystem of documentation and community resources to help you become a proficient Rust developer. In this section, we'll explore the various documentation sources and community platforms that can aid your Rust journey.

Official Rust Documentation

The official Rust documentation is a valuable resource for both beginners and experienced Rustaceans. It includes:

- **The Rust Programming Language Book**: This book, often referred to as the "Rust Book," is an excellent starting point for learning Rust. It covers the basics and advanced topics in an accessible manner. You can access it online at doc.rust-lang.org/book.

- **Rust Standard Library Documentation**: The Rust Standard Library (Std) is comprehensive, and its documentation provides details on all the standard types, functions, and modules. You can find it at doc.rust-lang.org/std.

- **Rust By Example**: If you prefer learning through practical examples, Rust By Example is a fantastic resource. It offers code snippets and explanations to demonstrate Rust concepts. Access it at doc.rust-lang.org/rust-by-example.

- **Rust Reference**: The Rust Reference is a detailed resource that dives deep into Rust's language features and syntax. It's useful when you need a precise understanding of Rust's inner workings. Find it at doc.rust-lang.org/reference.

Crates.io Documentation

Crates.io, the official Rust package registry, hosts a vast collection of Rust crates (libraries) contributed by the community. Each crate typically comes with its documentation. You can explore crates and their documentation at crates.io.

Community-Driven Resources

Rust has a vibrant and welcoming community that has created various resources to support learning and development:

- **Rust Forum**: The official Rust forum is a place to ask questions, share knowledge, and engage with the Rust community. Visit it at users.rust-lang.org.

- **Rust Reddit**: The r/rust subreddit is an active community where Rust developers discuss topics related to Rust, share projects, and seek help.

- **Rust Community Discord**: The Rust community hosts a Discord server where you can chat with fellow Rust enthusiasts, ask questions, and participate in discussions. Join at discord.gg/rust-lang.

- **Rust GitHub Repository**: Rust development happens on GitHub, and you can explore the Rust source code, file issues, and contribute to the language's development at github.com/rust-lang/rust.

- **Rust Weekly Newsletter**: The Rust Weekly newsletter summarizes recent happenings in the Rust world, including new releases, community projects, and articles.

- **Rust Learning**: The Rust Learning GitHub repository collects various resources, including books, articles, and courses, to help you learn Rust.

Editor and IDE Integration

Popular code editors and integrated development environments (IDEs) like Visual Studio Code, IntelliJ IDEA, and Atom have Rust plugins and extensions that provide code completion, syntax highlighting, and debugging support. These tools make Rust development more accessible and productive.

In conclusion, Rust offers an extensive set of official documentation, community-driven resources, and a welcoming community that can support your Rust learning and development journey. Whether you prefer learning from books, online documentation, forums, or interactive examples, there are resources available to cater to your learning style. Don't hesitate to engage with the Rust community, ask questions, and explore the multitude of crates available on crates.io to enhance your Rust projects.

7.4 Integrating Rust with Other Languages

Rust's interoperability with other programming languages is a powerful feature that allows you to leverage existing codebases and libraries from different languages while enjoying the safety and performance benefits of Rust. In this section, we'll explore how Rust can be integrated with other languages and some common use cases.

Foreign Function Interface (FFI)

Rust's Foreign Function Interface (FFI) enables seamless interaction with libraries written in C and other languages. FFI allows Rust to call functions from external libraries and vice versa.

To use FFI in Rust, you'll need to declare external functions using the extern keyword and provide their signatures. Here's an example of using FFI to call a C function:

```
extern "C" {
    fn some_c_function(arg1: i32, arg2: i32) -> i32;
}

fn main() {
    let result = unsafe { some_c_function(10, 20) };
    println!("Result from C function: {}", result);
}
```

This code snippet demonstrates how to call a C function named some_c_function from Rust. The extern "C" block specifies that we're interacting with C code.

Rust Bindings

When integrating Rust with other languages, you may need to create Rust bindings for foreign functions or libraries. Rust bindings are Rust code that wraps and provides a Rust-friendly API to foreign code.

Tools like bindgen can automatically generate Rust bindings for C or C++ libraries. You can use it by adding the bindgen crate to your Cargo.toml and configuring it to generate bindings for the desired header file.

Interoperability with C++

While Rust's FFI is primarily designed for C interoperability, you can also interface with C++ libraries using some additional considerations. Typically, you'll need to create a C-compatible wrapper around your C++ code and expose the desired functionality through a C API.

WebAssembly Integration

Rust can be compiled to WebAssembly (Wasm), allowing you to run Rust code in web browsers and interact with JavaScript. This is especially useful for performance-critical web applications and libraries.

To compile Rust to Wasm, you can use the `wasm-pack` tool, which simplifies the process of building and packaging Wasm modules.

Python Integration

Rust can be integrated with Python through various mechanisms, such as:

- **PyO3**: PyO3 is a Rust crate that enables you to create Python modules in Rust. It provides a convenient way to expose Rust code to Python.

- **RustPython**: RustPython is an alternative implementation of Python in Rust. While it's not a direct integration, it showcases Rust's capabilities in implementing programming languages.

Node.js Integration

You can also integrate Rust with Node.js, a popular JavaScript runtime. Tools like `neon-bindings` allow you to create Node.js modules using Rust.

C# and .NET Integration

Rust can be used in conjunction with C# and the .NET ecosystem through the use of interop mechanisms like P/Invoke for Windows or Rust's FFI for cross-platform compatibility.

Conclusion

Rust's interoperability capabilities make it a versatile language for integrating with existing codebases and ecosystems. Whether you need to interact with C libraries, work with other languages like Python or JavaScript, or compile to WebAssembly, Rust provides the tools and flexibility to seamlessly integrate with various environments and ecosystems.

7.5 Building and Publishing Your Own Crate

One of the significant advantages of Rust is its package management system, Cargo, which allows you to create, publish, and share your own Rust libraries and applications as crates. In this section, we'll explore the process of building your own crate, structuring it effectively, and publishing it to crates.io, the official Rust package registry.

Creating a New Crate

To start building your crate, you can use Cargo's built-in tools. Here's how you can create a new Rust crate:

```
# Create a new Rust crate named "my_crate"
cargo new my_crate
```

This command creates a new directory named "my_crate" with the necessary files and folder structure for your crate.

Structuring Your Crate

A well-structured crate follows Rust's conventions and best practices. Here are some important files and folders in a typical crate structure:

- **src/**: This directory contains your crate's source code. Rust source files usually have the .rs extension and are located here.

- **Cargo.toml**: This file is the manifest for your crate and specifies its metadata, dependencies, and build configuration.

- **README.md**: It's a good practice to include a README file that provides information about your crate, its purpose, and how to use it.

- **LICENSE**: This file specifies the license under which your crate is distributed. It's essential to choose a suitable open-source license for your project.

Writing Your Crate

You can start writing your Rust code in the src/ directory. Define your public API by marking the relevant functions, structs, and traits as pub. Users of your crate will only be able to access the public items.

Here's a simple example of a crate that defines a function to calculate the factorial of a number:

```rust
// src/lib.rs
pub fn factorial(n: u64) -> u64 {
    if n == 0 || n == 1 {
        1
    } else {
        n * factorial(n - 1)
    }
}
```

Adding Dependencies

If your crate depends on external libraries or crates, you can specify them in the Cargo.toml file under the [dependencies] section. For example, if you depend on the rand crate:

```toml
[dependencies]
rand = "0.8"
```

Building and Testing Your Crate

You can build your crate using the `cargo build` command and test it using the `cargo test` command. These commands compile your crate and run its tests, ensuring everything works as expected.

```
# Build your crate
cargo build
```

```
# Test your crate
cargo test
```

Publishing Your Crate

Once your crate is ready, you can publish it to crates.io, Rust's official package registry. To publish, you need a crates.io account and use the following command:

```
# Publish your crate to crates.io
cargo publish
```

This command will package and upload your crate to the registry, making it available for others to use.

Versioning Your Crate

It's essential to follow semantic versioning (SemVer) principles when releasing new versions of your crate. This ensures that users can update their dependencies without fear of breaking changes.

Conclusion

Building and publishing your own Rust crate allows you to contribute to the Rust ecosystem, share your libraries and applications, and collaborate with other Rust developers. By following best practices, structuring your crate effectively, and publishing it on crates.io, you can make your code accessible and valuable to the wider Rust community.

Chapter 8: Functional Programming in Rust

8.1 Principles of Functional Programming

Functional programming is a programming paradigm that treats computation as the evaluation of mathematical functions and avoids changing state and mutable data. It focuses on immutability, first-class functions, and higher-order functions. Rust, although not a purely functional language, supports functional programming concepts and can be used to write functional code. In this section, we'll explore the principles of functional programming and how they apply to Rust.

Immutability

Immutability is a fundamental concept in functional programming. It means that once a data structure is created, it cannot be modified. In Rust, you can achieve immutability by using the let keyword to create variables that cannot be reassigned. For example:

```
let x = 42; // Immutable variable
```

To work with mutable data, you can use the mut keyword:

```
let mut y = 10; // Mutable variable
y = 20; // Valid because 'y' is mutable
```

Immutable data reduces the risk of unintended side effects and makes code easier to reason about.

First-Class and Higher-Order Functions

In functional programming, functions are first-class citizens, which means they can be treated as values. Rust supports first-class functions, allowing you to assign functions to variables, pass them as arguments to other functions, and return them from functions.

```
fn add(a: i32, b: i32) -> i32 {
    a + b
}

let sum = add; // Assigning the 'add' function to 'sum'
let result = sum(5, 7); // Calling 'sum' as a regular function
```

Higher-order functions are functions that take other functions as arguments or return them as results. They are a powerful feature in functional programming, enabling you to write more concise and reusable code.

Pure Functions

Pure functions are functions that always produce the same output for the same input and have no side effects. They are a cornerstone of functional programming and contribute to code predictability and testability. Rust encourages writing pure functions by default. For example:

```rust
fn pure_function(x: i32) -> i32 {
    x * 2
}
```

Immutable Data Structures

Functional programming often relies on immutable data structures to manage and manipulate data. In Rust, you can use data structures like Vec or HashMap in an immutable way by cloning and creating new instances rather than modifying existing ones.

```rust
let original = vec![1, 2, 3];
let modified = original.clone(); // Create a new immutable 'Vec'
```

Pattern Matching

Pattern matching is a powerful feature in Rust that aligns with functional programming principles. It allows you to destructure and match data structures, making it easier to work with complex data.

```rust
fn process_data(data: Option<i32>) {
    match data {
        Some(value) => println!("Received data: {}", value),
        None => println!("No data available"),
    }
}
```

Conclusion

Functional programming principles can improve code readability, maintainability, and reliability. Rust's support for immutability, first-class and higher-order functions, pure functions, and pattern matching makes it a suitable choice for writing functional-style code. By incorporating these principles into your Rust projects, you can take advantage of the benefits of functional programming while leveraging Rust's safety and performance.

8.2 Iterators and Closures

In functional programming, iterators and closures play a significant role in enabling concise and expressive code for working with collections of data. Rust provides robust support for both iterators and closures, making it a powerful language for functional programming. In this section, we'll explore how iterators and closures work in Rust and how they can be applied in functional-style code.

Iterators in Rust

An iterator is an abstraction that represents a sequence of elements and provides methods for processing those elements one at a time. Rust's standard library includes various iterators that work with collections like arrays, vectors, and iterators themselves.

To create an iterator from a collection, you can use the iter() method. For example, let's create an iterator for a vector of numbers:

```
let numbers = vec![1, 2, 3, 4, 5];
let mut iter = numbers.iter(); // Create an iterator
```

You can use iterator methods like map, filter, and fold to perform transformations and computations on the elements of the iterator. For instance, to double each element in the vector:

```
let doubled: Vec<i32> = numbers.iter().map(|x| x * 2).collect();
```

Closures in Rust

Closures in Rust are anonymous functions that can capture and manipulate variables from their surrounding scope. They are defined using the |parameters| body syntax. Closures are often used with iterators to define custom behavior for processing elements.

Here's an example of a closure that filters out even numbers from a vector:

```
let numbers = vec![1, 2, 3, 4, 5];
let evens: Vec<i32> = numbers.into_iter().filter(|x| x % 2 == 0).collect();
```

Closures can capture variables by reference or by value, depending on their behavior and how they are used. This flexibility allows you to write expressive and efficient code.

Chaining Iterators and Closures

One of the strengths of Rust's iterator and closure system is the ability to chain operations together. You can apply multiple transformations and filters in a single expression, making your code more concise and readable.

```
let numbers = vec![1, 2, 3, 4, 5];
let result: Vec<i32> = numbers
    .iter()
    .map(|x| x * 2)
    .filter(|x| x % 4 == 0)
    .collect();
```

By chaining operations, you can express complex data manipulations in a declarative and functional style.

Laziness and Evaluation

Rust's iterators are lazy, meaning they only compute elements as needed. This laziness can lead to more efficient code, especially when working with large data sets. The computation is deferred until you request elements, which allows you to avoid unnecessary work.

Conclusion

Iterators and closures are essential tools for writing functional-style code in Rust. They enable you to work with collections in a concise and expressive manner, applying transformations and filters as needed. Rust's support for laziness and efficient evaluation makes it a strong choice for functional programming tasks involving data manipulation. By mastering these concepts, you can write code that is both readable and performant in Rust.

8.3 Functional Design Patterns

Functional design patterns are reusable solutions to common problems in functional programming. These patterns help you write cleaner, more maintainable code by encapsulating common idioms and practices. In Rust, you can apply functional design patterns to create elegant solutions for various tasks. In this section, we'll explore some functional design patterns and how they can be implemented in Rust.

1. Map and Reduce

The **Map and Reduce** pattern is a fundamental functional programming concept. It involves applying a transformation function (Map) to each element of a collection and then aggregating the results using a combining function (Reduce). In Rust, you can achieve this pattern using iterators and closures.

Here's an example that calculates the sum of squares of numbers in a vector:

```
let numbers = vec![1, 2, 3, 4, 5];
let sum_of_squares = numbers.iter().map(|x| x * x).fold(0, |acc, x| acc + x);
```

2. Pipe

The **Pipe** pattern allows you to compose multiple functions or transformations together, creating a pipeline of operations. In Rust, you can implement a pipe-like pattern using method chaining with iterators and closures. This approach promotes code readability and modularity.

```
let numbers = vec![1, 2, 3, 4, 5];
let result = numbers
    .iter()
    .map(|x| x * 2)
    .filter(|x| x % 4 == 0)
    .collect::<Vec<i32>>();
```

3. Memoization

Memoization is a pattern where you cache the results of expensive function calls to avoid redundant computations. In Rust, you can use closures and the `lazy_static` crate to implement memoization.

```rust
#[macro_use]
extern crate lazy_static;

use std::collections::HashMap;

lazy_static! {
    static ref FIB_CACHE: HashMap<u64, u64> = {
        let mut cache = HashMap::new();
        cache.insert(0, 0);
        cache.insert(1, 1);
        cache
    };
}

fn fib(n: u64) -> u64 {
    if let Some(&result) = FIB_CACHE.get(&n) {
        return result;
    }

    let result = fib(n - 1) + fib(n - 2);
    FIB_CACHE.insert(n, result);
    result
}
```

4. Currying and Partial Application

Currying and **Partial Application** are techniques for transforming functions with multiple arguments into functions that take one argument at a time. In Rust, you can achieve this using closures and nested functions.

```rust
fn add(x: i32) -> impl Fn(i32) -> i32 {
    move |y| x + y
}

let add_five = add(5);
let result = add_five(10); // Result is 15
```

5. Monads

Monads are design patterns used to encapsulate sequencing of operations and handling of potential errors or side effects. While Rust doesn't have built-in monads like some functional languages, you can implement monad-like patterns using Result and Option types.

```rust
fn divide(a: f64, b: f64) -> Result<f64, String> {
    if b == 0.0 {
        Err("Division by zero".to_string())
    } else {
        Ok(a / b)
    }
}

let result = divide(10.0, 2.0)
    .and_then(|x| divide(x, 5.0))
    .and_then(|x| divide(x, 2.0));
```

These are just a few examples of functional design patterns that can be applied in Rust. By using these patterns, you can write more expressive and maintainable code, taking full advantage of Rust's functional programming capabilities.

8.4 Functional Data Structures

Functional data structures are a critical component of functional programming, emphasizing immutability and pure functions. These data structures enable you to work with data in a functional way, preserving the original data while creating new modified versions. In Rust, you can implement functional data structures that adhere to the principles of immutability and functional programming. In this section, we will explore some common functional data structures and their usage in Rust.

1. Immutable Lists

Immutable lists are a fundamental functional data structure. They represent a collection of elements where once created, the list cannot be modified. Instead, operations on the list return new lists with the desired changes. In Rust, you can implement an immutable list using a custom data structure or use existing libraries like im-rs.

```rust
extern crate im;
use im::Vector;

let list = Vector::new().push(1).push(2).push(3);
let modified_list = list.push(4);
```

2. Persistent Maps

A persistent map is a key-value data structure that allows efficient insertion, deletion, and lookup operations while maintaining immutability. In Rust, you can use libraries like im-rs or implement your persistent map with custom code.

```rust
extern crate im;
use im::HashMap;
```

```
let map = HashMap::new().insert("key1", 1).insert("key2", 2);
let modified_map = map.remove("key1");
```

3. Option and Result

Option and Result types in Rust are functional data structures that represent values that
may or may not exist (Option) or operations that may succeed or fail (Result). These types
encourage handling potential errors or missing values in a functional way.

```
fn divide(a: f64, b: f64) -> Option<f64> {
    if b == 0.0 {
        None
    } else {
        Some(a / b)
    }
}
```

```
let result = divide(10.0, 2.0)
    .and_then(|x| divide(x, 5.0))
    .and_then(|x| divide(x, 2.0));
```

4. Functional Queues

Functional queues are data structures that provide efficient enqueue and dequeue
operations while preserving immutability. You can implement functional queues in Rust
using a combination of VecDeque and cloning.

```
use std::collections::VecDeque;

struct FunctionalQueue<T> {
    enqueue: VecDeque<T>,
    dequeue: VecDeque<T>,
}

impl<T> FunctionalQueue<T> {
    fn enqueue(&self, value: T) -> Self {
        let mut new_enqueue = self.enqueue.clone();
        new_enqueue.push_back(value);
        Self {
            enqueue: new_enqueue,
            dequeue: self.dequeue.clone(),
        }
    }

    fn dequeue(&self) -> Option<(T, Self)> {
        if let Some(front) = self.dequeue.front() {
            let mut new_dequeue = self.dequeue.clone();
            new_dequeue.pop_front();
            Some((front.clone(), Self {
```

```
                enqueue: self.enqueue.clone(),
                dequeue: new_dequeue,
            }))
        } else if !self.enqueue.is_empty() {
            let mut new_dequeue = self.enqueue.clone();
            new_dequeue.pop_front();
            Some((self.dequeue.front().unwrap().clone(), Self {
                enqueue: new_dequeue,
                dequeue: VecDeque::new(),
            }))
        } else {
            None
        }
    }
}
}
```

These functional data structures and patterns enable you to write code that is more predictable, easier to reason about, and better suited for concurrent or parallel programming. By embracing functional programming principles in Rust, you can create robust and maintainable applications.

8.5 Leveraging Rust's Functional Features

Rust is a versatile language that allows you to leverage functional programming features alongside its low-level control and systems programming capabilities. In this section, we'll explore how Rust supports functional programming and how you can make the most of these features in your projects.

1. First-Class Functions

Rust treats functions as first-class citizens, meaning you can pass them as arguments to other functions, return them from functions, and store them in data structures. This feature is essential for functional programming, allowing you to create higher-order functions and design more modular and reusable code.

```
fn apply_operation(operation: fn(i32, i32) -> i32, a: i32, b: i32) -> i32 {
    operation(a, b)
}

fn add(a: i32, b: i32) -> i32 {
    a + b
}

fn multiply(a: i32, b: i32) -> i32 {
    a * b
}
```

```rust
let result = apply_operation(add, 2, 3); // Result: 5
```

2. Closures

Closures in Rust are anonymous functions that capture variables from their surrounding scope. They are a powerful tool for creating concise and expressive code. You can use closures to implement functional-style operations like mapping, filtering, and reducing collections.

```rust
let numbers = vec![1, 2, 3, 4, 5];
let doubled: Vec<i32> = numbers.iter().map(|&x| x * 2).collect(); // Result:
[2, 4, 6, 8, 10]
```

3. Iterators

Rust's iterators allow you to work with collections in a functional way. You can chain various iterator methods to perform transformations and operations on collections. This approach promotes a declarative and functional style of code.

```rust
let numbers = vec![1, 2, 3, 4, 5];
let sum: i32 = numbers.iter().filter(|&&x| x % 2 == 0).map(|&x| x * 2).sum();
// Result: 12
```

4. Pattern Matching

Pattern matching is a powerful feature in Rust that aligns with functional programming principles. You can use match expressions to destructure and match data patterns, enabling more expressive and safer code.

```rust
enum Color {
    Red,
    Green,
    Blue,
}

fn print_color(color: Color) {
    match color {
        Color::Red => println!("It's red"),
        Color::Green => println!("It's green"),
        Color::Blue => println!("It's blue"),
    }
}
```

5. Immutability

Rust encourages immutability by default, making it easy to create code that adheres to functional programming principles. Immutable data structures and variables reduce side effects and make your code more predictable.

```
let x = 5;
let y = x; // y is a copy of x, and x remains unchanged
```

By incorporating these functional programming features into your Rust code, you can write more concise, maintainable, and expressive applications while still benefiting from Rust's safety and performance advantages. Whether you're working on a small project or a large-scale application, understanding and using these features can significantly enhance your Rust programming experience.

Chapter 9: Rust for Web Development

9.1 Introduction to Web Assembly and Rust

Web development is a rapidly evolving field, and Rust has made its mark as a viable language for building web applications. One of the key aspects of Rust's involvement in web development is its support for WebAssembly (Wasm). In this section, we'll explore what WebAssembly is, why it matters for web development, and how Rust plays a crucial role in this domain.

What is WebAssembly (Wasm)?

WebAssembly is an open standard that defines a portable binary code format for web applications. It allows high-performance execution of code on web browsers. Unlike JavaScript, which is traditionally used for web development, WebAssembly is a low-level binary instruction format that is designed to be a compilation target for high-level programming languages like Rust, C/C++, and others.

WebAssembly offers several advantages for web developers:

1. **Performance:** WebAssembly code runs at near-native speed in modern web browsers, making it ideal for computationally intensive tasks and applications that require real-time responsiveness.

2. **Security:** It provides a sandboxed execution environment, ensuring that code cannot access sensitive browser APIs directly. This enhances web application security.

3. **Language Agnostic:** WebAssembly is not tied to a specific programming language, making it versatile. Developers can choose the language that best suits their needs.

Rust and WebAssembly

Rust is particularly well-suited for WebAssembly for several reasons:

1. **Memory Safety:** Rust's ownership system ensures memory safety, which is crucial for web applications running in the browser. This prevents common programming errors like null pointer dereferences and buffer overflows.

2. **Performance:** Rust's focus on performance aligns perfectly with the goals of WebAssembly. Rust code compiles to efficient and optimized WebAssembly binaries.

3. **Bindings:** Rust provides tools and libraries for creating WebAssembly bindings, allowing you to interact seamlessly between Rust and JavaScript. This enables the use of existing JavaScript libraries in your Rust-based web applications.

4. **Ecosystem:** Rust has a growing ecosystem of WebAssembly-related libraries and tools, making it easier to get started with web development using Rust.

Getting Started with Rust and WebAssembly

To begin developing web applications with Rust and WebAssembly, you'll need to set up your development environment. Follow these steps to get started:

1. **Install Rust:** If you haven't already, install Rust by following the instructions on the official Rust website (https://www.rust-lang.org/).

2. **Install WebAssembly Target:** Rust has a WebAssembly target that you can add to your toolchain using the `rustup` command. Use the following command to install the WebAssembly target:

    ```
    rustup target add wasm32-unknown-unknown
    ```

3. **Choose a Web Framework:** Rust has several web frameworks and libraries that you can use for web development. Some popular options include Actix, Rocket, and Yew (for frontend development).

4. **Create Your Project:** Use Cargo, Rust's package manager, to create a new Rust project for your web application. You can use the `wasm-pack` tool to set up a new project that includes WebAssembly support.

    ```
    cargo generate --git https://github.com/rustwasm/wasm-pack-template
    ```

5. **Write Rust Code:** Write your Rust code for the web application, keeping in mind the interaction between Rust and JavaScript using WebAssembly bindings.

6. **Build and Bundle:** Use `wasm-pack` to build and bundle your Rust code into a WebAssembly module.

7. **Integrate with JavaScript:** You can create a JavaScript wrapper to load and interact with your WebAssembly module in the browser.

8. **Test and Deploy:** Test your web application locally, and when you're ready, deploy it to a web server.

Rust's integration with WebAssembly opens up exciting possibilities for web development. It allows developers to leverage Rust's performance, safety, and versatility while building web applications that run seamlessly in modern web browsers. Whether you're working on frontend or backend web development, Rust and WebAssembly provide a powerful combination for web developers to explore and utilize.

9.2 Building Web Applications with Rust

Web development with Rust has gained popularity due to its strong focus on safety, performance, and a growing ecosystem of libraries and frameworks. In this section, we will delve into building web applications using Rust, covering key concepts and tools.

Choosing a Web Framework

Rust offers several web frameworks to choose from, each with its own strengths and use cases. Here are a few popular options:

1. **Actix:** Actix is a high-performance, actor-based web framework for Rust. It is known for its speed and asynchronous handling of requests. Actix is a good choice for building scalable and fast web applications.

2. **Rocket:** Rocket is a web framework that focuses on developer productivity and ease of use. It comes with a rich set of features, including automatic data serialization, and is well-suited for rapid development.

3. **Tide:** Tide is a minimalistic web framework that provides asynchronous and composable middleware. It's designed to be flexible and works well for building RESTful APIs and services.

4. **Yew:** If you're interested in frontend web development with Rust, Yew is a Rust framework for building client-side web applications using WebAssembly. It allows you to write both frontend and backend code in Rust.

Choosing the right framework depends on your project requirements, your familiarity with Rust, and your preferences for performance and development speed.

Dependency Management with Cargo

Cargo, Rust's package manager, plays a crucial role in managing dependencies for your web application. You can specify dependencies in your project's `Cargo.toml` file and use Cargo commands to fetch and manage them. This makes it easy to include third-party libraries and packages in your project.

Here's an example of specifying a dependency in a `Cargo.toml` file:

```
[dependencies]
actix-web = "4.0"
serde = "1.0"
```

In this example, we're specifying dependencies on the Actix web framework and the Serde serialization library.

Handling HTTP Requests and Routes

Web applications need to handle incoming HTTP requests and define routes to map those requests to specific functions or handlers. Most Rust web frameworks provide a straightforward way to do this.

For instance, in Actix, you can define a route and associate it with a handler function like this:

```rust
use actix_web::{get, web, App, HttpResponse, HttpServer};

#[get("/hello")]
async fn hello() -> HttpResponse {
    HttpResponse::Ok().body("Hello, world!")
}

#[actix_rt::main]
async fn main() -> std::io::Result<()> {
    HttpServer::new(|| {
        App::new().service(hello)
    })
    .bind("127.0.0.1:8080")?
    .run()
    .await
}
```

In this example, the `hello` function is associated with the `/hello` route, and it returns a simple "Hello, world!" response.

Templating and Views

Web applications often require rendering HTML templates and dynamic views. Rust web frameworks offer various libraries for template rendering. For example, you can use the askama crate to handle templates in Actix:

```toml
[dependencies]
askama = "0.10"
```

```rust
use actix_web::{get, web, App, HttpResponse, HttpServer, Responder};
use askama::Template;

#[derive(Template)]
#[template(path = "hello.html")]
struct HelloTemplate {
    name: String,
}

#[get("/hello/{name}")]
async fn hello(web::Path(name): web::Path<String>) -> impl Responder {
    let template = HelloTemplate { name };
```

120

```rust
        HttpResponse::Ok().body(template.render().unwrap())
}

#[actix_rt::main]
async fn main() -> std::io::Result<()> {
    HttpServer::new(|| {
        App::new().service(hello)
    })
    .bind("127.0.0.1:8080")?
    .run()
    .await
}
```

In this example, the `askama` crate is used to render an HTML template with dynamic data.

Database Integration

Most web applications require database access for storing and retrieving data. Rust provides libraries like `diesel`, `sqlx`, and `rusqlite` for database integration. You can choose a database library based on your project's needs and the database system you plan to use.

Here's an example of using the `sqlx` crate to interact with a PostgreSQL database:

```rust
[dependencies]
sqlx = "0.5"

use sqlx::postgres::PgPool;
use sqlx::query;

#[tokio::main]
async fn main() -> Result<(), Box<dyn std::error::Error>> {
    let pool = PgPool::connect("postgres://username:password@localhost/databa
se").await?;

    let result = query!("SELECT name FROM users WHERE id = $1", 1)
        .fetch_one(&pool)
        .await?;

    let name: String = result.name;
    println!("User's name: {}", name);

    Ok(())
}
```

In this example, we connect to a PostgreSQL database using `sqlx` and execute a query.

Frontend Development with Yew

If you're building a web application with a frontend component, Rust's Yew framework allows you to write client-side code in Rust and compile it to WebAssembly. This provides a consistent and type-safe way to build both frontend and backend components of your web application.

Yew follows a component-based architecture similar to popular JavaScript frontend libraries like React. You can define reusable components and manage their state.

Here's a simple example of a Yew component:

```rust
use yew::prelude::*;

struct Model {
    link: ComponentLink<Self>,
    count: i32,
}

enum Msg {
    Increment,
    Decrement,
}

impl Component for Model {
    type Message = Msg;
    type Properties = ();
```

9.3 Rust in Backend Development

Rust's versatility extends to backend development, making it a compelling choice for building server-side applications and services. In this section, we'll explore how Rust can be used effectively for backend development, covering key aspects and tools.

Building HTTP Services

One of the fundamental aspects of backend development is handling HTTP requests and serving responses. Rust provides several libraries and frameworks for building HTTP services, making it easier to create robust and efficient web applications.

Using Hyper

Hypertext Transfer Protocol (HTTP) is the foundation of web communication. Hyper is a popular Rust library for building HTTP clients and servers. It offers a low-level, asynchronous API for handling HTTP connections and requests.

Here's a simple example of using Hyper to create an HTTP server:

```rust
use hyper::service::{make_service_fn, service_fn};
use hyper::{Body, Request, Response, Server};
```

```rust
async fn handle_request(_req: Request<Body>) -> Result<Response<Body>, hyper:
:Error> {
    Ok(Response::new(Body::from("Hello, Rust!")))
}

#[tokio::main]
async fn main() -> Result<(), Box<dyn std::error::Error>> {
    let addr = ([127, 0, 0, 1], 8080).into();
    let make_svc = make_service_fn(|_conn| {
        async { Ok::<_, hyper::Error>(service_fn(handle_request)) }
    });

    let server = Server::bind(&addr).serve(make_svc);
    println!("Listening on http://{}", addr);

    server.await?;

    Ok(())
}
```

In this example, we create an HTTP server using Hyper, define a request handler function (handle_request), and bind the server to a specific address.

Leveraging Actix-web

Actix-web is a powerful and high-performance web framework built on top of Actix, designed for asynchronous web applications. It simplifies the development of web services by providing abstractions for routing, middleware, and request handling.

Here's a basic Actix-web example:

```rust
use actix_web::{get, web, App, HttpResponse, HttpServer, Responder};

#[get("/hello")]
async fn hello() -> impl Responder {
    HttpResponse::Ok().body("Hello, Actix-web!")
}

#[actix_rt::main]
async fn main() -> Result<(), actix_web::Error> {
    HttpServer::new(|| {
        App::new().service(hello)
    })
    .bind("127.0.0.1:8080")?
    .run()
    .await?;

    Ok(())
}
```

In this Actix-web example, we define a route /hello and a handler function hello to respond with "Hello, Actix-web!" when accessed.

Cargo, Rust's package manager, simplifies dependency management for backend projects. You can specify dependencies in the Cargo.toml file, allowing you to include libraries and crates in your project effortlessly.

Here's an example Cargo.toml section for adding dependencies:

```
[dependencies]
actix-web = "3.5"
sqlx = "0.5"
tokio = { version = "1", features = ["full"] }
```

In this example, we specify dependencies on Actix-web, SQLx for database access, and Tokio for asynchronous runtime support.

Database Integration

Backend applications often require database access for storing and retrieving data. Rust offers various database libraries and ORMs (Object-Relational Mapping) to work with different database systems, including PostgreSQL, MySQL, SQLite, and more.

Using the SQLx library, here's how you can connect to a PostgreSQL database:

```
[dependencies]
sqlx = "0.5"
tokio = { version = "1", features = ["full"] }

use sqlx::postgres::PgPool;
use sqlx::query;

#[tokio::main]
async fn main() -> Result<(), Box<dyn std::error::Error>> {
    let pool = PgPool::connect("postgres://username:password@localhost/database").await?;

    let result = query!("SELECT name FROM users WHERE id = $1", 1)
        .fetch_one(&pool)
        .await?;

    let name: String = result.name;
    println!("User's name: {}", name);

    Ok(())
}
```

In this example, we connect to a PostgreSQL database, execute a query, and retrieve data using SQLx.

Middleware and Authentication

Backend applications often require middleware for tasks like authentication, request logging, and error handling. Rust's web frameworks, including Actix-web, provide middleware support to streamline these tasks.

You can add middleware to your Actix-web application like this:

```rust
use actix_web::{App, HttpResponse, HttpServer, middleware};

#[actix_rt::main]
async fn main() -> Result<(), actix_web::Error> {
    HttpServer::new(|| {
        App::new()
            .wrap(middleware::Logger::default())
            .service(/* your routes */)
    })
    .bind("127.0.0.1:8080")?
    .run()
    .await?;

    Ok(())
}
```

In this example, we use Actix-web's `middleware::Logger` to log incoming requests.

Testing and Deployment

Rust promotes a strong testing culture, and there are several testing libraries and tools available. You can write unit tests, integration tests, and even perform property-based testing using libraries like `proptest`.

For deployment, Rust applications can be compiled to standalone executables, making it easy to deploy on various platforms. Docker containers and orchestration tools like Kubernetes are commonly used for deploying Rust backend applications.

Rust's combination of safety, performance, and a growing ecosystem of libraries and frameworks makes it a promising choice for backend development. Whether you're building RESTful APIs, microservices, or full-fledged web applications, Rust provides the tools and reliability needed to succeed in backend development.

In the next section, we'll explore how Rust can be integrated with JavaScript and used in frontend web development.

9.4 Integrating Rust with JavaScript

Integrating Rust with JavaScript opens up exciting possibilities for web development. WebAssembly (Wasm) is at the heart of this integration, allowing you to run Rust code directly in web browsers and Node.js. In this section, we'll explore how to seamlessly blend the power of Rust with the ubiquity of JavaScript.

WebAssembly and Rust

WebAssembly is a binary instruction format that enables high-performance execution of code on web browsers. Rust is well-suited for compiling to WebAssembly, thanks to its low-level capabilities and memory safety features.

To start, you'll need the Rust toolchain with WebAssembly support, which can be installed using rustup:

```
rustup target add wasm32-unknown-unknown
```

With WebAssembly support added, you can compile Rust code to Wasm using the wasm-pack tool. Here's a basic example of Rust code compiled to WebAssembly:

```rust
// src/lib.rs
use wasm_bindgen::prelude::*;

#[wasm_bindgen]
pub fn add(a: i32, b: i32) -> i32 {
    a + b
}
```

In this example, we define a simple Rust function add that takes two integers and returns their sum.

To compile this code to WebAssembly, you can run:

```
wasm-pack build --target web
```

This command generates a Wasm binary and JavaScript bindings that make it accessible from JavaScript.

Using Rust in a Web Application

Once you've compiled your Rust code to WebAssembly, you can use it in a web application alongside JavaScript. Here's how you can use the add function in a simple HTML file:

```html
<!-- index.html -->
<!DOCTYPE html>
<html lang="en">
<head>
    <meta charset="UTF-8">
    <title>Rust + JavaScript Example</title>
</head>
```

```
<body>
    <h1>Result: <span id="result"></span></h1>
    <script type="module">
        import init, { add } from './pkg/your_crate_name.js';

        async function run() {
            await init();

            const result = add(5, 3);
            document.getElementById('result').textContent = result;
        }

        run();
    </script>
</body>
</html>
```

In this HTML file, we import the generated JavaScript module and use the add function to perform addition. The result is displayed on the web page.

JavaScript Interoperability

Rust and JavaScript can communicate seamlessly using WebAssembly. You can pass various data types between the two languages, including integers, strings, and even custom structs. WebAssembly's JavaScript API (WebAssembly.instantiate) facilitates communication between JavaScript and WebAssembly modules.

Additionally, Rust has excellent support for the wasm-bindgen library, which simplifies the interaction between Rust and JavaScript. You can annotate Rust code with #[wasm_bindgen] to generate JavaScript bindings automatically.

Leveraging JavaScript Libraries

One of the advantages of integrating Rust with JavaScript is the ability to leverage existing JavaScript libraries and frameworks. You can use Rust for performance-critical parts of your application while still enjoying the extensive JavaScript ecosystem.

For example, you can use popular frontend frameworks like React, Vue.js, or Angular to build user interfaces while relying on Rust for computationally intensive tasks or complex algorithms.

Node.js and Rust

WebAssembly isn't limited to web browsers. You can also use Rust with Node.js by leveraging the Node.js WASI runtime. This allows you to write server-side code in Rust, providing high performance and memory safety.

In conclusion, integrating Rust with JavaScript through WebAssembly opens up a wide range of possibilities in web development. Whether you're building frontend applications, backend services, or cross-platform desktop applications, combining the strengths of Rust and JavaScript can lead to more robust and performant solutions. The Rust and WebAssembly ecosystem continues to grow, providing exciting opportunities for developers to explore this powerful combination.

9.5 Case Studies: Successful Rust Web Projects

In this section, we'll explore some real-world case studies of successful web projects that have leveraged Rust for different purposes. These examples demonstrate the versatility and effectiveness of Rust in various web development scenarios.

1. Rocket: A Web Framework for Rust

Rocket is a popular web framework for Rust that has gained recognition for its elegant and intuitive API design. It provides a robust foundation for building web applications with features like routing, request handling, and templating.

Rocket's use of Rust's strong type system ensures that many common web-related bugs are caught at compile-time. This makes it a great choice for building secure and reliable web services. Rocket has been employed in various projects, including RESTful APIs, web applications, and microservices.

2. Warp: Asynchronous Web Services

Warp is another web framework for Rust, focusing on asynchronous programming. It leverages Rust's async/await syntax and provides a highly performant foundation for building asynchronous web services.

Warp's use of async I/O operations allows it to handle a large number of concurrent connections efficiently. It's often used in applications where low-latency and high-throughput are essential, such as real-time communication platforms, gaming servers, and data streaming services.

3. Actix: Actor-Based Framework

Actix is an actor-based framework for building highly concurrent and efficient web applications in Rust. It is designed around the actor model, making it suitable for applications requiring fine-grained concurrency control.

Actix is frequently used in applications that must handle thousands of simultaneous connections, such as chat applications, IoT platforms, and financial trading systems. Its lightweight actors and asynchronous message-passing architecture contribute to its high performance.

4. Parcel: Web Application Bundler

Parcel is a blazing-fast web application bundler written in Rust. While not a complete web framework, it plays a crucial role in optimizing frontend web development workflows.

Parcel's Rust core allows it to bundle and optimize JavaScript, CSS, and other web assets with exceptional speed. Developers use Parcel to enhance the performance of web applications by automatically generating efficient bundles and leveraging Rust's performance advantages in asset processing.

5. Sonic: Fast Search Server

Sonic is an open-source search server built with Rust. It provides full-text search capabilities with impressive speed and minimal resource consumption.

Sonic is often used as a backend service for web applications that require fast and efficient searching, such as e-commerce platforms, content management systems, and data analytics tools. Its Rust-based implementation ensures high performance, making it an attractive choice for search-intensive applications.

These case studies demonstrate the diverse applications of Rust in web development. From building web frameworks and asynchronous services to optimizing asset bundling and enabling lightning-fast search, Rust continues to gain traction in the web development ecosystem due to its performance, safety guarantees, and thriving ecosystem of libraries and frameworks. Developers can choose the right Rust tool for their specific web project needs, knowing that they are building on a foundation of speed, reliability, and security.

Chapter 10: Cross-Platform Development with Rust

10.1 Rust on Different Operating Systems

In this section, we'll explore how Rust can be utilized for cross-platform development, allowing you to write code that runs seamlessly on various operating systems. Rust's focus on safety, performance, and portability makes it an excellent choice for creating cross-platform applications.

Why Cross-Platform Development?

Cross-platform development involves writing code that can be executed on multiple operating systems, such as Windows, macOS, Linux, and even mobile platforms like Android and iOS. There are several compelling reasons for considering cross-platform development:

1. **Reach a Wider Audience**: By targeting multiple platforms, you can reach a broader audience of users, which is especially important for applications like mobile apps and desktop software.

2. **Code Reusability**: Cross-platform development encourages code reusability. You can share a significant portion of your codebase across different platforms, reducing development time and maintenance efforts.

3. **Consistent User Experience**: Cross-platform development ensures a consistent user experience across various devices and operating systems. Users expect applications to look and behave similarly on all platforms.

4. **Cost-Efficiency**: Developing separate codebases for each platform can be costly and time-consuming. Cross-platform solutions can save both time and money.

Rust for Cross-Platform Development

Rust's design principles align well with the requirements of cross-platform development:

- **Safety**: Rust's strong type system and ownership model ensure memory safety and prevent common programming errors. This is crucial for developing stable cross-platform applications.

- **Performance**: Rust's emphasis on zero-cost abstractions and low-level control allows you to optimize your code for each platform's specific requirements, delivering high-performance applications.

- **Portability**: Rust's standard library and ecosystem provide abstractions for platform-specific functionality. Libraries like `std::fs` abstract file system operations, making it easier to write cross-platform code.

- **Ecosystem**: Rust's package manager, Cargo, simplifies dependency management and allows you to integrate external libraries seamlessly, many of which offer cross-platform support.

To develop cross-platform applications in Rust, you can leverage the following tools and approaches:

1. **Cross-Compilation**: Rust supports cross-compilation, allowing you to build binaries for different target platforms from your development machine. This is useful when targeting platforms like embedded systems or different operating systems.

   ```
   # Cross-compile for a specific target
   cargo build --target=x86_64-pc-windows-msvc
   ```

2. **Cross-Platform Libraries**: Rust has libraries and frameworks like winit for windowing and input, gfx-rs for graphics, and tokio for asynchronous programming that provide cross-platform abstractions, making it easier to write code that works across OSes.

3. **WebAssembly (Wasm)**: Rust's integration with WebAssembly allows you to run Rust code in web browsers, extending cross-platform capabilities to the web. This is valuable for web applications and games.

4. **GUI Development**: For cross-platform GUI development, Rust offers libraries like druid and gtk-rs, which allow you to create desktop applications with native user interfaces on multiple OSes.

5. **Mobile Development**: Rust can be used in combination with tools like Flutter (for mobile apps) and React Native to write cross-platform mobile applications.

6. **Embedded Systems**: Rust's low-level control and memory safety features make it suitable for developing embedded systems software that needs to run on various microcontroller platforms.

7. **C/C++ Interoperability**: Rust can interface with C/C++ libraries, enabling the use of platform-specific libraries and system calls.

In the following chapters, we will delve into these approaches and tools in more detail, exploring how Rust can be leveraged for cross-platform development across a wide range of scenarios. Whether you're building desktop applications, web services, or embedded systems, Rust's versatility and safety guarantees will prove invaluable in your cross-platform endeavors.

10.2 Rust on Different Operating Systems: A Practical Guide

In this section, we will take a practical approach to utilizing Rust for cross-platform development by exploring how to write code that runs smoothly on various operating systems. We'll discuss platform-specific considerations, tools, and techniques to ensure your Rust applications are truly cross-platform.

Writing Cross-Platform Code

1. Platform-Dependent Logic

When writing cross-platform code, it's essential to identify platform-specific logic and handle it gracefully. Rust provides a way to conditionally compile code based on the target platform using cfg attributes:

```rust
fn main() {
    #[cfg(target_os = "windows")]
    println!("Hello from Windows!");

    #[cfg(target_os = "macos")]
    println!("Hello from macOS!");

    #[cfg(target_os = "linux")]
    println!("Hello from Linux!");
}
```

2. Handling File Paths

File paths are represented differently on various operating systems. Rust's std::path module provides cross-platform abstractions for working with file paths. Use the std::path::Path type for path manipulation:

```rust
use std::path::Path;

fn main() {
    let path = Path::new("my_folder");

    #[cfg(target_os = "windows")]
    let file = path.join("file.txt");

    #[cfg(not(target_os = "windows"))]
    let file = path.join("file.txt");

    println!("File path: {:?}", file);
}
```

3. Dealing with Line Endings

Text files may have different line endings on Windows (\r\n) and Unix-based systems (\n). Rust's std::fs module provides functions to handle this:

132

```rust
use std::fs::File;
use std::io::{BufRead, BufReader};

fn main() -> std::io::Result<()> {
    let file = File::open("my_file.txt")?;
    let reader = BufReader::new(file);

    for line in reader.lines() {
        #[cfg(target_os = "windows")]
        let line = line?.replace("\r", "");

        println!("{}", line);
    }

    Ok(())
}
```

Using Cross-Platform Libraries

Rust's ecosystem offers various cross-platform libraries to simplify cross-platform development:

- **winit**: Provides a unified API for window creation and input handling, supporting Windows, macOS, and Linux.

- **gfx-rs**: An abstraction over graphics APIs like Vulkan, DirectX, and Metal, enabling cross-platform graphics programming.

- **tokio**: A framework for asynchronous programming that works on different platforms, facilitating network and I/O operations.

- **druid**: A native GUI toolkit for Rust that allows you to create cross-platform desktop applications with native user interfaces.

Cross-Compiling Rust Code

Rust's support for cross-compilation allows you to build binaries for different target platforms. You can specify the target platform using the --target flag with cargo build:

```
# Cross-compile for Windows from a Linux development machine
cargo build --target=x86_64-pc-windows-msvc
```

Conclusion

Writing cross-platform Rust code involves understanding platform-specific differences and using conditional compilation and cross-platform libraries to ensure your code runs smoothly on various operating systems. Rust's safety and performance characteristics make it an excellent choice for cross-platform development, whether you're building desktop applications, web services, or embedded systems. In the upcoming chapters, we'll delve deeper into specific cross-platform scenarios and tools, helping you become proficient in creating Rust applications that can truly cross boundaries.

10.3 GUI Development with Rust: Building Cross-Platform Interfaces

Graphical User Interfaces (GUIs) are a crucial part of many software applications, from desktop applications to mobile apps. Developing GUIs with Rust allows you to create cross-platform interfaces that can run on Windows, macOS, Linux, and more. In this section, we'll explore GUI development in Rust and discuss various libraries and tools that simplify the process.

Choosing a GUI Framework

When it comes to GUI development in Rust, you have several options to choose from. Some of the most notable GUI frameworks and libraries include:

1. **druid**: druid is a native GUI toolkit for Rust that aims to provide a modern and native feel across different platforms. It supports Windows, macOS, and Linux.

2. **gtk-rs**: If you prefer using the GTK toolkit for building cross-platform GUIs, gtk-rs provides Rust bindings for GTK. It's a solid choice for Linux and can be used on other platforms with some limitations.

3. **iced**: iced is a cross-platform GUI library that focuses on simplicity and performance. It's suitable for building user interfaces in Rust that work on multiple platforms, including the web.

4. **qt (Rust Qt Binding)**: If you're familiar with Qt and want to use it with Rust, there are Rust bindings available for the Qt framework. Qt is known for its robustness and cross-platform capabilities.

Developing a Cross-Platform GUI Application

Let's explore a basic example of creating a cross-platform GUI application using the druid library. First, you'll need to add druid as a dependency in your Cargo.toml:

```
[dependencies]
druid = "0.8"
```

Now, you can create a simple "Hello, Rust GUI!" application using druid:

```rust
use druid::widget::Label;
use druid::{AppLauncher, LocalizedString, Widget, WindowDesc};

fn main() {
    // Describe the main window
    let main_window = WindowDesc::new(ui_builder)
```

134

```
        .title(LocalizedString::new("Hello, Rust GUI!").with_placeholder("Hel
lo, Rust GUI!"));

    // Launch the application
    AppLauncher::with_window(main_window)
        .use_simple_logger()
        .launch("Hello, Rust GUI!")
        .expect("Failed to launch application");
}

fn ui_builder() -> impl Widget<String> {
    Label::new("Hello, Rust GUI!")
}
```

In this example, we create a simple window with a "Hello, Rust GUI!" label using the druid library. When you run this application, it will display a basic cross-platform GUI window.

Considerations for Cross-Platform GUI Development

While developing cross-platform GUIs with Rust is possible and powerful, it's essential to consider a few factors:

- **Platform Differences**: Each platform has its own UI guidelines and design principles. Ensure that your GUI elements and layouts adhere to the platform's conventions for the best user experience.

- **Performance**: GUI applications may have different performance requirements on various platforms. Optimize your code and use libraries that provide good performance on all target platforms.

- **Testing**: Test your GUI application on different platforms to identify and fix platform-specific issues and ensure a consistent user experience.

- **User Feedback**: Encourage user feedback to improve your application's cross-platform compatibility and address any platform-specific concerns that users may have.

In conclusion, Rust provides several options for developing cross-platform GUI applications, and you can choose a GUI framework or library based on your preferences and project requirements. Building cross-platform GUIs with Rust allows you to create versatile and efficient applications that can run on various operating systems, opening up opportunities for widespread use and adoption.

10.4 Mobile Development with Rust: Building Cross-Platform Mobile Apps

Mobile app development is a thriving field, and Rust has not been left behind. You can leverage Rust's power and safety to build cross-platform mobile applications for both iOS and Android. In this section, we'll explore some of the tools and libraries that enable mobile development in Rust and discuss best practices for building cross-platform mobile apps.

Mobile Development with Rust and Flutter

One of the most popular ways to build cross-platform mobile apps using Rust is by using Google's Flutter framework. Flutter is known for its fast development and expressive UI, making it an excellent choice for mobile development. Thanks to the `flutter_rust_bridge` crate, you can integrate Rust code into your Flutter project seamlessly.

Here's a high-level overview of how you can set up a Flutter project with Rust integration:

1. **Install Flutter**: Begin by installing Flutter and setting up your development environment.

2. **Create a Flutter Project**: Use the `flutter create` command to create a new Flutter project.

3. **Add Rust Code**: Inside your Flutter project, you can add Rust code and functions using the `flutter_rust_bridge` crate. This crate provides a bridge between your Flutter Dart code and Rust code.

4. **Build and Run**: You can build and run your Flutter app as usual. When you invoke Rust functions from Dart, the `flutter_rust_bridge` crate handles the communication.

Building a Cross-Platform Mobile App with Rust and Flutter

Let's create a simple example of a cross-platform mobile app that calculates the sum of two numbers using Rust and Flutter. First, make sure you have Flutter installed and set up:

```
flutter create rust_flutter_app
cd rust_flutter_app
```

Now, add the `flutter_rust_bridge` crate to your `pubspec.yaml` file:

```
dependencies:
  flutter:
    sdk: flutter
  flutter_rust_bridge: ^0.1.0 # Check for the latest version on pub.dev
```

Create a Rust file named `lib.rs` inside the `lib` directory of your Flutter project:

```
// lib/lib.rs

#[no_mangle]
pub extern "C" fn add_numbers(a: i32, b: i32) -> i32 {
```

```
    a + b
}
```

In your Flutter Dart code, you can call the Rust function add_numbers like this:

```
import 'package:flutter_rust_bridge/flutter_rust_bridge.dart';

void main() {
  runApp(MyApp());
}

class MyApp extends StatelessWidget {
  @override
  Widget build(BuildContext context) {
    final result = RustBridge.addNumbers(10, 5); // Calls the Rust function
    return MaterialApp(
      home: Scaffold(
        appBar: AppBar(
          title: Text('Rust Flutter App'),
        ),
        body: Center(
          child: Text('Sum: $result'),
        ),
      ),
    );
  }
}
```

In this example, we've integrated Rust and Flutter to build a simple cross-platform mobile app that calculates and displays the sum of two numbers.

Considerations for Mobile Development in Rust

While mobile development with Rust offers many advantages, including safety and performance, it's essential to keep the following considerations in mind:

- **Platform Differences**: iOS and Android have different UI and design guidelines. Ensure that your app's user interface and user experience (UI/UX) follow the guidelines for each platform.

- **Testing**: Thoroughly test your app on both iOS and Android devices to catch platform-specific issues and ensure a consistent user experience.

- **Performance**: Optimize your Rust code to meet the performance requirements of mobile devices, which may have limited resources compared to desktop systems.

- **Cross-Platform Plugins**: Many Flutter plugins are available for common tasks. However, if you need to use platform-specific features, you may need to write platform-specific code or find a suitable plugin.

In conclusion, Rust's integration with Flutter makes it possible to build cross-platform mobile apps that combine Rust's safety and performance with Flutter's expressive UI. This approach enables you to create mobile applications that work seamlessly on both iOS and Android devices, opening up opportunities for broader app distribution and user reach.

10.5 Building Cross-Platform Applications with Rust

Cross-platform development is becoming increasingly popular as it allows developers to write code that runs on multiple operating systems with minimal modifications. Rust is well-suited for cross-platform application development, thanks to its focus on performance, safety, and portability. In this section, we'll explore various approaches and tools for building cross-platform applications with Rust.

1. Cross-Platform Development Frameworks

1.1. GTK

The GTK (GIMP Toolkit) library is a popular choice for building cross-platform graphical user interfaces (GUIs) in Rust. It provides native-looking interfaces on multiple platforms, including Linux, macOS, and Windows. You can use the gtk-rs crate to access GTK's functionality from Rust.

Here's a simple example of creating a GTK application in Rust:

```rust
use gtk::prelude::*;
use gtk::{Label, Window, WindowType};

fn main() {
    gtk::init().expect("Failed to initialize GTK.");

    let window = Window::new(WindowType::Toplevel);
    window.set_title("GTK Rust App");
    window.set_default_size(320, 240);

    let label = Label::new(Some("Hello, Rust GTK!"));

    window.add(&label);

    window.show_all();

    window.connect_delete_event(|_, _| {
        // Terminate the GTK main loop on window close
        gtk::main_quit();
        Inhibit(false)
    });
```

```
    gtk::main();
}
```

1.2. Qt

Qt is a popular cross-platform application framework known for its versatility and wide range of supported platforms. You can use the `qmetaobject-rs` crate to build Qt-based applications in Rust. Qt supports various platforms, including Linux, macOS, Windows, and mobile platforms like Android and iOS.

2. Web-Based Cross-Platform Apps

2.1. WebAssembly (Wasm)

WebAssembly is a binary instruction format that enables high-performance execution of code on web browsers. Rust has excellent support for compiling to WebAssembly, making it possible to create cross-platform web applications using Rust as the backend.

You can use the `wasm-pack` tool to build WebAssembly modules from Rust code. Frontend web frameworks like React, Vue.js, or Angular can then use these modules for the user interface.

3. Mobile Cross-Platform Apps

3.1. Flutter

Flutter, a Google UI toolkit, allows you to build natively compiled applications for mobile, web, and desktop from a single codebase. While it primarily uses Dart for development, you can integrate Rust into your Flutter project using the `flutter_rust_bridge` crate.

This approach enables you to share business logic and libraries across different platforms while creating platform-specific user interfaces.

4. Game Development

4.1. Amethyst

Amethyst is a data-driven game engine written in Rust, designed for flexibility and performance. It supports cross-platform game development for various target platforms, including Windows, macOS, Linux, and the web (through WebAssembly).

With Amethyst, you can create games that run seamlessly on multiple operating systems without extensive code changes.

5. Desktop Applications

5.1. Electron

Electron allows you to build cross-platform desktop applications using web technologies such as HTML, CSS, and JavaScript. While Electron primarily uses JavaScript, you can include Rust components using Rust's FFI (Foreign Function Interface).

This approach lets you leverage Rust's performance and safety within an Electron-based application.

6. Command-Line Tools

Rust is an excellent choice for building cross-platform command-line tools. Thanks to its focus on performance and safety, you can create efficient and reliable tools that work on various operating systems without major modifications.

In conclusion, Rust's versatility and ecosystem make it a strong contender for cross-platform application development. Whether you're targeting desktop, mobile, web, or other platforms, Rust provides the tools and libraries to help you build high-quality, cross-platform applications efficiently.

Chapter 11: Rust for Systems Programming

Section 11.1: Rust in Operating Systems Development

Rust has gained significant attention and adoption in the field of operating systems development. Traditional operating systems are often implemented in low-level languages like C or C++, which can lead to memory safety issues and security vulnerabilities. Rust, with its focus on memory safety and system-level programming, offers a compelling alternative for building operating systems.

The Advantages of Rust in OS Development

Rust brings several advantages to the table when it comes to operating systems development:

1. **Memory Safety**: One of the most critical aspects of OS development is ensuring memory safety. Rust's ownership system and strict borrowing rules help prevent common memory-related bugs such as null pointer dereferences, buffer overflows, and data races. This results in more robust and secure operating systems.

2. **Zero-cost Abstractions**: Rust provides high-level abstractions without incurring a runtime performance penalty. This is essential for building efficient and responsive operating systems.

3. **Concurrency**: Rust's concurrency model, including the use of threads and asynchronous programming, is well-suited for handling the parallelism required in modern operating systems.

4. **Static Analysis**: Rust's borrow checker performs static analysis on the code, catching many errors at compile-time, which can help prevent bugs from making their way into the final operating system.

5. **Interoperability**: Rust offers excellent interoperability with C, making it possible to integrate Rust components into existing C-based operating systems or libraries.

Use Cases for Rust in OS Development

Rust is being used in various operating system-related projects and research. Some notable use cases include:

- **Redox**: Redox is a microkernel-based operating system written entirely in Rust. It aims to provide a safe and efficient foundation for systems programming.

- **Tock**: Tock is an embedded operating system designed for running multiple concurrent applications on low-power, memory-constrained IoT devices. It leverages Rust's memory safety and concurrency features.

- **Cloud-Hypervisor**: Cloud-Hypervisor is an open-source hypervisor for cloud workloads. It uses Rust for its virtual machine monitor (VMM) component to ensure security and stability.

- **Fuchsia**: While not exclusively Rust-based, Google's Fuchsia OS includes components written in Rust for various system-level tasks.

- **Research**: Rust is also used in academic research to explore new approaches to operating system design with a focus on security and reliability.

Challenges and Considerations

Despite its advantages, using Rust in operating systems development presents some challenges:

- **Lack of Mature Libraries**: While Rust's ecosystem is growing rapidly, it may still lack some mature libraries and components commonly used in traditional OS development.

- **Tooling**: The development tooling for Rust in the context of operating systems may not be as mature as that for C/C++. Developers may need to create custom tooling and workflows.

- **Complexity**: Building an operating system is a complex task, and Rust's strict rules and safety checks may add an additional layer of complexity. However, this can pay off in terms of long-term maintainability and security.

In summary, Rust's focus on memory safety, zero-cost abstractions, and concurrency make it an attractive choice for operating systems development. It is already being used in various projects and research efforts, demonstrating its potential to reshape the way we build and maintain operating systems.

Section 11.2: Network Programming with Rust

Rust is becoming increasingly popular for network programming due to its emphasis on safety, performance, and concurrency. Network applications require robust handling of data transmission, protocol parsing, and concurrent connections, all of which can benefit from Rust's features.

Building Network Servers

Rust provides libraries and abstractions for building network servers. The most commonly used library for this purpose is the std::net module, which offers essential networking primitives like sockets and network addressing. You can create TCP or UDP servers using Rust's standard library.

Here's a simple example of a TCP server in Rust:

```rust
use std::net::{TcpListener, TcpStream};
use std::io::{Read, Write};

fn handle_client(mut stream: TcpStream) {
    let mut buffer = [0; 512];
    stream.read(&mut buffer).unwrap();
    let request = String::from_utf8_lossy(&buffer);
    println!("Received request: {}", request);

    let response = "Hello, client!\n";
    stream.write_all(response.as_bytes()).unwrap();
}

fn main() {
    let listener = TcpListener::bind("127.0.0.1:8080").unwrap();

    for stream in listener.incoming() {
        match stream {
            Ok(stream) => {
                std::thread::spawn(|| {
                    handle_client(stream);
                });
            }
            Err(e) => {
                eprintln!("Error accepting connection: {}", e);
            }
        }
    }
}
```

This code creates a simple TCP server that listens on `127.0.0.1:8080` and handles incoming connections in separate threads.

Asynchronous Networking

Rust's asynchronous programming model is well-suited for network applications with high concurrency requirements. The `async`/`await` syntax, combined with libraries like `tokio` or `async-std`, enables efficient handling of thousands of concurrent connections with minimal overhead.

Here's an example of an asynchronous TCP server using the `tokio` library:

```rust
use tokio::net::TcpListener;
use tokio::io::{AsyncReadExt, AsyncWriteExt};

#[tokio::main]
async fn main() -> Result<(), Box<dyn std::error::Error>> {
    let listener = TcpListener::bind("127.0.0.1:8080").await?;
```

```rust
    println!("Server listening on 127.0.0.1:8080");

    while let Ok((mut socket, _)) = listener.accept().await {
        tokio::spawn(async move {
            let mut buffer = [0; 512];
            if let Err(e) = socket.read(&mut buffer).await {
                eprintln!("Failed to read from socket: {}", e);
                return;
            }

            let response = "Hello, client!\n";
            if let Err(e) = socket.write_all(response.as_bytes()).await {
                eprintln!("Failed to write to socket: {}", e);
                return;
            }
        });
    }

    Ok(())
}
```

This code demonstrates an asynchronous TCP server using `tokio`, which can handle multiple clients concurrently without blocking.

Protocol Parsing and Serialization

Network programming often involves working with various protocols, such as HTTP, WebSocket, or custom binary protocols. Rust's ecosystem offers libraries for parsing and serializing data in different formats, making it easier to implement network protocols.

For instance, you can use the hyper library for building HTTP servers and clients, and serde for efficient serialization and deserialization of structured data.

Rust's combination of safety, performance, and concurrency support makes it an excellent choice for network programming, from simple servers to high-performance network applications. It ensures that you can build reliable and efficient networking software while minimizing the risk of common programming errors.

Section 11.3: File System and I/O Operations

Rust offers powerful and safe abstractions for performing file system and I/O operations. Whether you need to read and write files, manipulate directories, or work with standard input/output streams, Rust's standard library provides the tools you need while maintaining safety and reliability.

Reading and Writing Files

To read and write files in Rust, you can use the std::fs module. It provides functions for opening, reading, and writing files in a safe and efficient manner. Here's an example of reading a file:

```rust
use std::fs::File;
use std::io::prelude::*;

fn main() -> std::io::Result<()> {
    let mut file = File::open("example.txt")?;
    let mut contents = String::new();
    file.read_to_string(&mut contents)?;
    println!("File contents: \n{}", contents);
    Ok(())
}
```

In this code, we open a file named "example.txt," read its contents into a String, and print them to the console. Rust's error handling (Result) ensures that any potential errors are properly handled.

Writing to a file is similarly straightforward:

```rust
use std::fs::File;
use std::io::prelude::*;

fn main() -> std::io::Result<()> {
    let mut file = File::create("output.txt")?;
    let data = "Hello, Rust!";
    file.write_all(data.as_bytes())?;
    println!("Data written to output.txt");
    Ok(())
}
```

This code creates a file named "output.txt" and writes the string "Hello, Rust!" to it.

Directory Operations

To work with directories, you can use the std::fs module as well. It provides functions for creating, removing, and navigating directories. Here's an example of creating a directory:

```rust
use std::fs;

fn main() -> std::io::Result<()> {
    fs::create_dir("new_directory")?;
    println!("Directory 'new_directory' created.");
    Ok(())
}
```

This code creates a new directory named "new_directory" in the current working directory.

Standard Input and Output

Rust's standard library also provides convenient abstractions for working with standard input (stdin) and standard output (stdout). You can use the std::io module to read user input and write output to the console.

Here's a simple example of reading user input and echoing it back:

```
use std::io;

fn main() {
    let mut input = String::new();
    println!("Enter some text:");
    io::stdin().read_line(&mut input).expect("Failed to read input");
    println!("You entered: {}", input);
}
```

This code prompts the user for input, reads the input from stdin, and then prints it back to the console.

Rust's I/O and file system operations, combined with its strong safety guarantees, make it a robust choice for developing applications that require file handling, directory manipulation, or user interaction. Whether you're building a file converter, a command-line utility, or a text editor, Rust's I/O capabilities have you covered while ensuring that your code remains secure and reliable.

Section 11.4: Building Command-Line Tools

Command-line tools are an essential part of system administration, automation, and development workflows. Rust excels at building command-line applications due to its performance, safety, and ecosystem of libraries. In this section, we will explore how to create command-line tools using Rust.

Command-Line Argument Parsing

Rust provides several libraries for parsing command-line arguments. One of the most popular choices is the clap library, which allows you to define command-line arguments and options with ease. Here's a basic example:

```
extern crate clap;

use clap::{App, Arg};

fn main() {
    let matches = App::new("My CLI Tool")
        .version("1.0")
```

```
        .author("Your Name")
        .about("A simple command-line tool")
        .arg(
            Arg::with_name("input")
                .short("i")
                .long("input")
                .value_name("FILE")
                .help("Input file")
                .takes_value(true),
        )
        .arg(
            Arg::with_name("output")
                .short("o")
                .long("output")
                .value_name("FILE")
                .help("Output file")
                .takes_value(true),
        )
        .get_matches();

    if let Some(input_file) = matches.value_of("input") {
        println!("Input file specified: {}", input_file);
    }

    if let Some(output_file) = matches.value_of("output") {
        println!("Output file specified: {}", output_file);
    }
}
```

In this example, we define a simple command-line tool that accepts input and output file paths as arguments. The clap library helps us parse and handle these arguments efficiently.

Running External Commands

Sometimes, you may need to execute external commands from your Rust application. The std::process::Command struct allows you to do this easily. Here's a basic example of running an external command:

```
use std::process::Command;

fn main() {
    let output = Command::new("ls")
        .arg("-l")
        .output()
        .expect("Failed to execute command");

    println!("Command output:\n{}", String::from_utf8_lossy(&output.stdout));
}
```

In this code, we run the `ls -l` command and capture its output. You can replace `"ls"` with any other command you want to execute.

Creating Interactive Tools

Rust also provides libraries for building interactive command-line tools. Libraries like `dialoguer` and `crossterm` help you create text-based user interfaces with prompts, menus, and input validation. These can be useful for building tools that require user interaction.

Here's a simple example using the `dialoguer` library to prompt the user for input:

```rust
extern crate dialoguer;

use dialoguer::Input;

fn main() {
    let username: String = Input::new()
        .with_prompt("Enter your username")
        .interact_text()
        .unwrap();

    println!("Hello, {}!", username);
}
```

In this code, we use the `Input` prompt from `dialoguer` to request and display user input.

Building command-line tools with Rust allows you to leverage its performance and safety features while creating versatile and efficient tools for various purposes. Whether you need to automate tasks, interact with users, or integrate with existing systems, Rust provides the tools and libraries to make your command-line applications robust and reliable.

Section 11.5: Rust in High-Performance Computing

High-Performance Computing (HPC) involves solving complex problems that require significant computational power. Rust, known for its focus on performance and safety, has been gaining traction in the field of HPC. In this section, we will explore how Rust is used in high-performance computing and some of the advantages it offers.

Performance and Safety

One of the primary reasons Rust is gaining popularity in HPC is its ability to provide both high performance and memory safety. Rust's ownership system eliminates many common sources of bugs, such as null pointer dereferences and data races. This allows HPC developers to write code that runs efficiently without sacrificing safety.

Parallelism and Concurrency

Rust's strong support for parallelism and concurrency is another factor that makes it suitable for HPC. Rust provides features like threads, message passing, and atomic operations, which are essential for leveraging modern multi-core processors and distributed computing environments. The absence of a global interpreter lock (GIL), a common limitation in languages like Python, allows Rust to fully utilize the available hardware resources.

```rust
use std::thread;

fn main() {
    let thread_count = 4;
    let mut handles = vec![];

    for _ in 0..thread_count {
        let handle = thread::spawn(|| {
            // Code to be executed by each thread
        });
        handles.push(handle);
    }

    for handle in handles {
        handle.join().unwrap();
    }
}
```

In this example, we create and spawn multiple threads to perform parallel computation. Rust's built-in thread support simplifies the process of parallelizing tasks.

Interoperability

Rust's interoperability with C and other languages is crucial in HPC, where existing libraries and tools are often used. Rust can easily interface with C libraries through FFI (Foreign Function Interface), enabling HPC developers to leverage existing C code while benefiting from Rust's safety features.

SIMD and Vectorization

Single Instruction, Multiple Data (SIMD) operations are essential for HPC applications that perform data-intensive computations. Rust allows developers to use SIMD instructions through libraries like std::arch, providing fine-grained control over vectorization.

GPU Programming

Many HPC applications benefit from GPU acceleration. Rust has libraries like rust-cuda and rust-rocm that enable GPU programming, allowing developers to harness the power of GPUs for parallel computation.

```
extern crate rust_cuda;
use rust_cuda::prelude::*;
use rust_cuda::rustacuda::memory::DeviceBox;
use std::error::Error;

fn main() -> Result<(), Box<dyn Error>> {
    rust_cuda::init(CudaFlags::empty())?;

    let data = vec![1.0f32, 2.0f32, 3.0f32];
    let mut device_data = DeviceBox::new(&data)?;

    // Perform GPU computation here

    Ok(())
}
```

In this example, we demonstrate how to use the `rust-cuda` library to perform GPU computations with Rust.

Numerical Computing Libraries

Rust has several libraries for numerical computing, such as `ndarray`, `nalgebra`, and `statrs`. These libraries provide essential tools for HPC applications, including linear algebra, random number generation, and statistical analysis.

Rust's growing ecosystem, combined with its performance, safety, and concurrency features, makes it a compelling choice for high-performance computing. As the language continues to evolve and gain support for more HPC-specific features, its adoption in this field is likely to increase.

Chapter 12: Advanced Rust Programming Techniques

Section 12.1: Macros and Metaprogramming

In Rust, macros are a powerful metaprogramming feature that allows you to generate code at compile-time. Macros provide a way to write code that writes code, which can help reduce boilerplate, improve code organization, and enable code reuse. In this section, we will explore Rust macros and their applications.

What Are Macros?

Macros in Rust are similar to functions but operate at the syntactic level rather than the value level. They are defined using the macro_rules! keyword and can take patterns as input, which match against the code provided when invoking the macro. Macros use a declarative syntax to specify how code should be generated or transformed.

Macro Invocation

To invoke a macro, you use the macro_name! syntax, where macro_name is the name of the macro you want to use. Arguments can be passed to macros, and these arguments are processed within the macro definition to generate code.

```rust
macro_rules! greeting {
    ($name:expr) => {
        println!("Hello, {}!", $name);
    };
}

fn main() {
    greeting!("Alice");
    greeting!("Bob");
}
```

In this example, the greeting! macro takes an expression as an argument and generates code to print a greeting message with the provided name.

Code Generation

One common use case for macros is code generation. Macros can help generate repetitive code patterns, reducing the potential for errors and making code maintenance easier. For instance, you can create macros to define multiple similar functions or data structures with slight variations.

```rust
macro_rules! create_structs {
    ($($name:ident),*) => {
        $(struct $name { field: i32 })*
    };
}
```

```
create_structs!(A, B, C);

fn main() {
    let a = A { field: 42 };
    let b = B { field: 123 };
    let c = C { field: 7 };
}
```

Here, the `create_structs!` macro generates three struct definitions, A, B, and C, with a common field `field`. This eliminates the need to write each struct definition manually.

DRY (Don't Repeat Yourself) Principle

Macros are a valuable tool for adhering to the DRY (Don't Repeat Yourself) principle. They allow you to abstract repetitive code patterns into reusable macros, promoting cleaner and more maintainable code. Macros can be used to define custom domain-specific languages (DSLs) and simplify complex tasks.

Challenges and Pitfalls

While macros offer significant flexibility and power, they can also introduce complexity and make code harder to understand. It's important to use macros judiciously and document them well. Rust's macro system is hygienic, meaning it enforces a strict scope and avoids unintended variable shadowing and conflicts.

In summary, Rust macros are a powerful feature for code generation and metaprogramming. They enable developers to reduce code duplication, improve code organization, and create more expressive and concise code. However, they should be used with care and documented effectively to ensure maintainability and readability of the codebase.

Section 12.2: Advanced Traits and Type Systems

In this section, we will delve into advanced traits and the type system in Rust. While Rust's trait system and type system have already been introduced in previous chapters, this section explores more advanced concepts and patterns related to these fundamental aspects of the language.

Associated Types

Rust allows traits to define associated types, which are types that are associated with the trait but not specified until the trait is implemented. This feature is particularly useful when defining traits for data structures that can have different types for specific operations.

```rust
trait Stack {
    type Item;
    fn push(&mut self, item: Self::Item);
    fn pop(&mut self) -> Option<Self::Item>;
}

struct IntStack {
    data: Vec<i32>,
}

impl Stack for IntStack {
    type Item = i32;

    fn push(&mut self, item: i32) {
        self.data.push(item);
    }

    fn pop(&mut self) -> Option<i32> {
        self.data.pop()
    }
}
```

In this example, the Stack trait defines an associated type Item, which is the type of elements stored in the stack. The IntStack struct then implements this trait with i32 as the associated type.

Supertraits

Rust allows traits to inherit methods from other traits using supertraits. Supertraits specify that a trait must also implement another trait to be considered valid.

```rust
trait Printable {
    fn print(&self);
}

trait DebugPrintable: Printable {
    fn debug_print(&self);
}

struct MyStruct;

impl Printable for MyStruct {
    fn print(&self) {
        println!("Printing MyStruct");
    }
}

impl DebugPrintable for MyStruct {
    fn debug_print(&self) {
        println!("Debug Printing MyStruct");
```

153

```
        }
}
```

In this example, the DebugPrintable trait is a supertrait of Printable. This means that to implement DebugPrintable, a type must also implement Printable. The MyStruct type implements both traits.

Phantom types are types that have no runtime representation but are used to enforce constraints at compile time. They are often used in combination with traits to express complex relationships between types.

```
struct Meter;
struct Kilogram;

struct Measurement<T> {
    value: f64,
    _unit: std::marker::PhantomData<T>,
}

trait Unit {}

impl Unit for Meter {}
impl Unit for Kilogram {}

fn main() {
    let length: Measurement<Meter> = Measurement {
        value: 2.5,
        _unit: std::marker::PhantomData,
    };

    let weight: Measurement<Kilogram> = Measurement {
        value: 5.7,
        _unit: std::marker::PhantomData,
    };
}
```

In this example, the Measurement struct is parameterized by a type parameter T, which is used as a phantom type to represent units of measurement (e.g., Meter or Kilogram). This ensures that operations involving measurements are type-safe and units are not mixed up.

Advanced Type Constraints

Rust's type system allows you to specify complex constraints on generic types using trait bounds. This enables you to express intricate relationships between types and ensure that certain properties are upheld.

```
fn process<T: std::cmp::PartialOrd>(list: &[T]) -> T {
    let mut max = list[0];
```

```
    for &item in list.iter() {
        if item > max {
            max = item;
        }
    }
    max
}

fn main() {
    let numbers = vec![3, 7, 1, 9, 4, 2];
    let max_num = process(&numbers);
    println!("Max: {}", max_num);
}
```

In this example, the process function takes a slice of type T where T implements the PartialOrd trait, ensuring that elements in the list can be compared. This demonstrates how you can define precise type constraints for generic functions.

Advanced Traits and Type System Summary

Rust's advanced trait system and type system provide powerful tools for expressing complex relationships between types, ensuring type safety, and enabling flexible and reusable code. Associated types, supertraits, phantom types, and advanced type constraints are some of the features that allow you to create expressive and safe abstractions in your Rust programs. These concepts are crucial when designing libraries and frameworks and when dealing with complex domain-specific problems.

Section 12.3: Unsafe Rust for Low-Level Control

In this section, we explore the use of "unsafe" in Rust, a feature that allows you to bypass some of the language's safety guarantees to gain low-level control over your code. While Rust is known for its strong emphasis on safety and memory management, there are situations where you may need to break these rules to achieve specific goals. However, with great power comes great responsibility, and using "unsafe" should be approached with caution.

The "unsafe" Keyword

Rust's "unsafe" keyword opens a new realm of possibilities for developers. It allows you to perform operations that would typically be considered unsafe by the compiler, such as:

- Dereferencing raw pointers directly.
- Modifying mutable references while immutable references exist.
- Implementing unsafe traits.
- Interfacing with foreign functions or languages.

```rust
fn main() {
    let mut num = 42;

    // Creating a raw pointer to `num`
    let raw_ptr: *mut i32 = &mut num;

    // Dereferencing the raw pointer (unsafe)
    unsafe {
        *raw_ptr += 10;
    }

    println!("Modified num: {}", num);
}
```

In this example, we create a raw pointer to a mutable integer and modify it through the pointer using the "unsafe" block. This is an unsafe operation because it can lead to data races and memory safety issues if not used correctly.

Unsafe Functions and Blocks

You can define your own unsafe functions and blocks in Rust when you need to encapsulate unsafe operations. These blocks should be used sparingly and documented well to indicate the potential risks.

```rust
unsafe fn unsafe_function() {
    // Perform unsafe operations here
}

fn main() {
    unsafe {
        unsafe_function();
    }
}
```

Unsafe Traits and Implementations

Traits can also be marked as "unsafe" when their implementations involve unsafe operations. When implementing an unsafe trait, you must ensure that the trait's requirements are met while adhering to Rust's safety guarantees.

```rust
unsafe trait UnsafeTrait {
    fn unsafe_method(&self);
}

struct MyStruct;

unsafe impl UnsafeTrait for MyStruct {
    fn unsafe_method(&self) {
        // Implement the method with unsafe operations
```

```
        }
}
```

Safe Abstractions with Unsafe Code

While "unsafe" code is often associated with low-level operations, it can also be used to create safe abstractions and libraries. Libraries like the standard library and various crates leverage "unsafe" code internally to provide safe and efficient interfaces to users.

Guidelines for Using "unsafe"

When using "unsafe" in Rust, follow these guidelines:

1. Minimize the use of "unsafe" code and encapsulate it in well-documented functions or blocks.
2. Thoroughly understand the potential risks and verify that your code adheres to Rust's safety guarantees.
3. Avoid data races, null pointer dereferences, and buffer overflows.
4. Leverage safe abstractions and libraries whenever possible.
5. Use tools like "unsafe" linting and code analysis to catch potential issues.

"unsafe" code is a powerful tool in Rust that grants you fine-grained control and performance optimization opportunities. However, it should be wielded with care, and safety should always be a top priority.

Section 12.4: Optimizing Rust Code

Optimizing Rust code is an essential aspect of software development, especially when striving for better performance, reduced memory usage, or faster execution. Rust's emphasis on safety and control doesn't mean you have to sacrifice performance. In this section, we'll explore various techniques and best practices for optimizing Rust code.

Profiling and Benchmarking

Before diving into optimizations, it's crucial to identify performance bottlenecks accurately. Profiling tools like "cargo-profiler" and "perf" help you pinpoint where your code spends the most time. Rust also provides a built-in benchmarking framework with the "cargo bench" command to measure and compare the execution time of different code paths.

```
#![feature(test)]
extern crate test;

use test::Bencher;

fn expensive_computation(n: u64) -> u64 {
    // ... Code to benchmark
```

157

```
        n * 2
}

#[bench]
fn bench_expensive_computation(b: &mut Bencher) {
    b.iter(|| {
        expensive_computation(42);
    });
}
```

Data Structures and Algorithms

Choosing the right data structures and algorithms can significantly impact your code's performance. Rust's standard library provides efficient collections and algorithms, so leverage them when possible. Additionally, consider custom data structures tailored to your specific needs for optimal performance.

Profiling and Optimizing Hot Loops

Hot loops are portions of your code that consume a significant amount of CPU time. By carefully optimizing these sections, you can achieve substantial performance improvements. Techniques like loop unrolling, loop fusion, and branch prediction optimizations can be applied, but always profile first to identify bottlenecks accurately.

```
fn hot_loop(data: &[i32]) -> i32 {
    let mut sum = 0;
    for &num in data {
        // Optimized loop code
        sum += num;
    }
    sum
}
```

Compiler Optimization Flags

Rust's compiler, "rustc," offers various optimization flags that allow you to fine-tune code generation. The most common flags include "-C opt-level" to specify optimization levels and "-C target-cpu" to target a specific CPU architecture for optimizations.

```
# Compile with optimizations
$ rustc -C opt-level=3 -o my_program source.rs
```

Unsafe Code for Low-Level Optimization

In certain situations, you may need to resort to "unsafe" Rust for low-level optimization. However, this should be your last resort and should be approached with extreme caution. Ensure that the optimizations provide a significant performance boost and that safety is maintained.

Caching and Memoization

Caching and memoization can be effective techniques for avoiding redundant computations and reducing execution time. Rust provides libraries like "lazy_static" for static memoization and "dashmap" for concurrent caches.

```rust
lazy_static! {
    static ref CACHE: HashMap<u64, u64> = HashMap::new();
}

fn expensive_computation(n: u64) -> u64 {
    if let Some(result) = CACHE.get(&n) {
        return *result;
    }

    let result = n * 2;
    CACHE.insert(n, result);
    result
}
```

Avoiding Unnecessary Allocations

Minimizing memory allocations and deallocations can lead to significant performance improvements. Use stack-allocated variables when possible and consider reusing memory buffers to reduce allocation overhead.

Parallelism and Concurrency

Leveraging Rust's support for parallelism and concurrency can provide substantial performance boosts, especially on multi-core processors. Explore libraries like "rayon" for parallel processing and "async/await" for concurrent execution of asynchronous tasks.

Optimizing Rust code requires a combination of profiling, algorithmic improvements, compiler flags, and careful consideration of "unsafe" code. Keep in mind that premature optimization can lead to code complexity and reduced maintainability, so prioritize clarity and correctness before pursuing optimizations. Profiling should guide your optimization efforts to ensure they address the most critical performance bottlenecks.

Section 12.5: Exploring Rust's Type System

Rust boasts a robust and expressive type system that combines safety and flexibility, enabling developers to write efficient and reliable code. In this section, we delve into Rust's type system, exploring its key features and how they contribute to safer and more maintainable software.

159

Strong and Static Typing

Rust is known for its strong and static type system, which means that the type of every value is determined at compile-time and cannot be changed at runtime. This provides a high degree of safety by catching type-related errors before the code runs, reducing the risk of runtime crashes and errors.

```rust
fn main() {
    let x: i32 = 42;
    // The following line would result in a compile-time error:
    // let y: i32 = "hello";
}
```

Type Inference

Rust's type inference system allows developers to omit type annotations in many cases. The compiler can deduce the type of a variable based on its usage, making the code concise while preserving safety.

```rust
fn main() {
    let x = 42;   // Type i32 is inferred
    let y = "hello";   // Type &str is inferred
}
```

Ownership and Borrowing

Rust's ownership system ensures that memory is managed safely, preventing common bugs like null pointer dereferences and memory leaks. Ownership rules dictate how data can be shared or borrowed, enforcing strict compile-time checks.

```rust
fn main() {
    let s1 = String::from("hello");
    let s2 = s1;   // Ownership is moved to s2, s1 is invalidated
    // The following line would result in a compile-time error:
    // println!("{}", s1);
}
```

References and Borrowing

Rust allows multiple references to data without copying, as long as certain borrowing rules are followed. This enables efficient and safe sharing of data between different parts of the code.

```rust
fn main() {
    let s1 = String::from("hello");
    let len = calculate_length(&s1); // Pass a reference to s1
    println!("Length of '{}' is {}.", s1, len);
}

fn calculate_length(s: &String) -> usize {
```

```
    s.len()
}
```

Enums and Pattern Matching

Enums in Rust enable developers to define custom types with multiple possible values. Pattern matching allows you to handle different enum variants elegantly, making your code more readable and expressive.

```
enum TrafficLight {
    Red,
    Yellow,
    Green,
}

fn main() {
    let light = TrafficLight::Red;

    match light {
        TrafficLight::Red => println!("Stop!"),
        TrafficLight::Yellow => println!("Slow down!"),
        TrafficLight::Green => println!("Go!"),
    }
}
```

Traits and Polymorphism

Traits in Rust are similar to interfaces in other languages, allowing you to define a set of methods that types must implement. This concept of trait-based polymorphism enables generic programming and code reuse.

```
trait Printable {
    fn print(&self);
}

struct Circle {
    radius: f64,
}

impl Printable for Circle {
    fn print(&self) {
        println!("Circle with radius {}.", self.radius);
    }
}

fn main() {
    let circle = Circle { radius: 5.0 };
    circle.print();
}
```

Custom Types and Abstraction

Rust allows developers to create custom data types through structs, enums, and traits. This capability fosters abstraction, enabling you to model your domain with precision and build high-level abstractions that simplify complex systems.

```rust
struct Rectangle {
    width: u32,
    height: u32,
}

impl Rectangle {
    fn area(&self) -> u32 {
        self.width * self.height
    }
}

fn main() {
    let rect = Rectangle { width: 10, height: 20 };
    let area = rect.area();
    println!("Area of the rectangle is {} square units.", area);
}
```

Rust's type system, built around ownership, borrowing, and lifetimes, empowers developers to write safe, concurrent, and high-performance code. By understanding and mastering these features, you can take full advantage of Rust's expressive and efficient type system to build reliable software.

Chapter 13: Rust for Game Development

Section 13.1: Introduction to Game Development with Rust

Game development is an exciting field that combines creativity, engineering, and interactive storytelling. Rust, with its strong emphasis on safety and performance, is gaining popularity as a choice for game development. In this section, we'll introduce you to the world of game development with Rust, covering its advantages, tools, and libraries.

Why Rust for Game Development?
1. **Safety**: Safety is paramount in game development. Rust's ownership system and borrow checker help prevent common bugs like null pointer dereferences and buffer overflows, making it an ideal choice for systems that demand high reliability.

2. **Performance**: Games often require squeezing every bit of performance from the hardware. Rust's zero-cost abstractions and control over memory allocation allow you to write high-performance code without sacrificing safety.

3. **Concurrency**: Modern games often leverage multi-threading and parallelism to enhance performance. Rust's built-in support for concurrency and thread safety makes it well-suited for this task.

4. **Cross-Platform**: Rust's cross-platform capabilities make it easier to target multiple platforms, including Windows, macOS, Linux, and even WebAssembly. This reduces development effort and allows you to reach a broader audience.

5. **Ecosystem**: Rust has a growing ecosystem of game development libraries and tools. Crates like ggez, amethyst, and bevy provide game engines and frameworks that simplify game development tasks.

Getting Started with Rust Game Development

To embark on a Rust game development journey, you'll need to set up your development environment. Start by installing Rust and Cargo, the Rust package manager, if you haven't already. You can follow the official Rust installation guide for your platform.

Once Rust is set up, you can create a new Rust project for your game using Cargo:

```
cargo new my_game
cd my_game
```

This creates a new Rust project with the necessary directory structure and a default main.rs file.

Game Engines and Frameworks

Game development often involves complex tasks like rendering, input handling, and physics simulation. To simplify these tasks, Rust offers various game engines and frameworks:

- **ggez**: ggez is a simple and lightweight game framework for Rust. It provides a simple API for creating 2D games with minimal setup.

- **amethyst**: Amethyst is a data-driven game engine suitable for building complex and highly customizable games. It follows an entity-component-system (ECS) architecture.

- **bevy**: Bevy is a fast and modular ECS game engine designed for simplicity and flexibility. It is known for its ergonomic and expressive API.

- **piston**: Piston is a game engine with a focus on 2D games and multimedia applications. It provides various libraries for graphics, windowing, and more.

Game Development Resources

To become proficient in Rust game development, consider exploring the following resources:

- **Official Rust Game Development Book**: The official Rust Game Development book is a valuable resource for learning game development in Rust. It covers various aspects of game development and provides practical examples.

- **Community Forums and Discord**: Rust has an active game development community. You can join forums like the Rust Game Development Forum and the Rust GameDev subreddit, or engage with developers on Discord servers dedicated to Rust game development.

- **Online Tutorials and Courses**: Many online tutorials and courses focus on Rust game development. Platforms like Udemy and Coursera offer courses that can help you get started.

- **Open Source Games**: Studying open-source Rust games on platforms like GitHub can provide insights into real-world game development practices and codebases.

In the following sections of this chapter, we will explore various aspects of Rust game development, including graphics programming, user input handling, and building a simple game using a game engine or framework of your choice. Whether you're a beginner or an experienced game developer, Rust offers a robust and safe environment for creating captivating games.

Section 13.2: Rust Game Engines and Frameworks

Rust's ecosystem for game development has seen substantial growth, and it offers a variety of game engines and frameworks to choose from. These engines and frameworks aim to simplify the process of creating games by providing abstractions and tools for common game development tasks. In this section, we will explore some of the popular Rust game engines and frameworks.

ggez

ggez is a straightforward and lightweight game framework for Rust, designed to make 2D game development easy. It abstracts many low-level details and provides a simple API for handling game loops, input, graphics, and audio.

One of the notable features of ggez is its minimal setup. To create a game using ggez, you can start by defining a Game struct and implementing the EventHandler trait:

```rust
use ggez::{event, graphics, Context, GameResult};

struct MyGame {}

impl MyGame {
    fn new() -> Self {
        Self {}
```

```
        }
    }

    impl event::EventHandler for MyGame {
        fn update(&mut self, _ctx: &mut Context) -> GameResult {
            // Game logic goes here
            Ok(())
        }

        fn draw(&mut self, ctx: &mut Context) -> GameResult {
            // Drawing code goes here
            graphics::clear(ctx, graphics::BLACK);
            // Draw your game objects here
            graphics::present(ctx)?;
            Ok(())
        }
    }

    fn main() -> GameResult {
        let cb = ggez::ContextBuilder::new("my_game", "author")
            .window_setup(ggez::conf::WindowSetup::default().title("My Rust Game"
    ))
            .window_mode(ggez::conf::WindowMode::default().dimensions(800.0, 600.
    0));
        let (ctx, event_loop) = &mut cb.build()?;
        let game = &mut MyGame::new();
        event::run(ctx, event_loop, game)
    }
```

In the code snippet above, we define a basic game using ggez. We create a MyGame struct, implement the EventHandler trait to handle game events, and define the game logic and drawing code.

Amethyst

Amethyst is a data-driven game engine built in Rust. It is designed for building complex and highly customizable games and follows an entity-component-system (ECS) architecture.

Amethyst provides a robust set of features, including a powerful ECS framework, asset management, rendering, input handling, and more. With Amethyst, you can structure your game using entities, components, and systems, allowing for flexible and modular game development.

Creating a game with Amethyst typically involves defining entities and their associated components, writing systems to update game logic, and configuring the game's resources and assets. While Amethyst may have a steeper learning curve compared to simpler frameworks, it offers great flexibility and control over game development.

Bevy

Bevy is a relatively new and rapidly growing Rust game engine designed for simplicity and flexibility. It adopts an ECS architecture similar to Amethyst but focuses on providing an ergonomic and expressive API.

One of Bevy's strengths is its ease of use and clear documentation. Creating a basic game in Bevy involves defining entities, components, and systems in a straightforward manner. Bevy emphasizes code simplicity and readability, making it accessible for developers of all experience levels.

Here's a simple example of creating a game window and displaying a sprite in Bevy:

```rust
use bevy::prelude::*;

fn main() {
    App::build()
        .add_startup_system(setup.system())
        .add_startup_stage("game_setup", SystemStage::single(spawn_sprite.system()))
        .add_plugins(DefaultPlugins)
        .run();
}

fn setup(commands: &mut Commands) {
    commands
        .spawn(Camera2dBundle::default())
        .spawn(CameraUiBundle::default());
}

fn spawn_sprite(commands: &mut Commands) {
    commands
        .spawn(SpriteBundle {
            material: materials::Color::rgb(0.0, 0.7, 0.0).into(),
            sprite: Sprite::new(Vec2::new(100.0, 100.0)),
            transform: Transform::from_translation(Vec3::new(0.0, 0.0, 0.0)),
            ..Default::default()
        });
}
```

In this example, we create an application, set up a basic game window with cameras, and spawn a colored sprite using Bevy's concise API.

Other Options

Apart from ggez, Amethyst, and Bevy, there are several other Rust game engines and frameworks available, each with its own strengths and use cases. Some additional options include:

- **Piston**: Piston is a game engine focused on 2D game development and multimedia applications. It provides libraries for graphics, windowing, and more.

- **Macroquad**: Macroquad is a fast and easy-to-use game framework that supports both 2D and 3D graphics. It is designed for rapid development and prototyping.

When choosing a game engine or framework for your Rust game development project, consider your specific requirements, the complexity of your game, and your familiarity with the tools. Each engine or framework has its unique features and trade-offs, so

Section 13.3: Graphics Programming in Rust

Graphics programming is a fundamental aspect of game development, and Rust offers several libraries and frameworks for handling graphics tasks efficiently. In this section, we will explore the key aspects of graphics programming in Rust, including rendering, shaders, and 2D/3D graphics.

Rendering with OpenGL and Vulkan

Graphics rendering in Rust often involves using low-level graphics APIs like OpenGL or Vulkan. While these APIs are more complex compared to higher-level abstractions, they provide fine-grained control over the rendering process, making them suitable for performance-critical applications.

The gfx and ash libraries are commonly used for working with OpenGL and Vulkan in Rust. They provide Rust bindings to these APIs, allowing developers to interact with them using Rust's safety guarantees. These libraries are well-documented and have active communities, making them a solid choice for graphics programming.

```rust
extern crate ash;
use ash::version::{InstanceV1_0, EntryV1_0};

fn main() {
    // Initialize Vulkan
    let entry = ash::Entry::new().expect("Failed to load Vulkan entry");
    let app_name = CString::new("My Vulkan App").unwrap();
    let engine_name = CString::new("My Vulkan Engine").unwrap();

    let app_info = vk::ApplicationInfo {
        p_application_name: app_name.as_ptr(),
        p_engine_name: engine_name.as_ptr(),
        ..Default::default()
    };

    let create_info = vk::InstanceCreateInfo {
        p_application_info: &app_info,
```

```
        ..Default::default()
    };

    let instance = unsafe {
        entry
            .create_instance(&create_info, None)
            .expect("Failed to create Vulkan instance")
    };

    // Further Vulkan initialization and rendering code goes here
}
```

In the code snippet above, we initialize Vulkan using the ash library. This is a simplified example and doesn't include rendering code, but it demonstrates the basic setup required for graphics programming with Vulkan in Rust.

Graphics Shaders

Shaders are essential for defining how graphics are rendered in a game or application. In Rust, you can write shaders in GLSL (OpenGL Shading Language) for OpenGL or SPIR-V (Standard Portable Intermediate Representation) for Vulkan.

To compile and use shaders in Rust, you can use libraries like glsl-to-spirv for translating GLSL shaders to SPIR-V, and then load and use them in your graphics pipeline. Shader code is often written in separate files and loaded at runtime.

```
use std::fs::File;
use std::io::Read;

fn load_shader(file_path: &str) -> Vec<u8> {
    let mut file = File::open(file_path).expect("Failed to open shader file")
;
    let mut shader_code = Vec::new();
    file.read_to_end(&mut shader_code).expect("Failed to read shader file");
    shader_code
}

fn main() {
    // Load vertex and fragment shaders
    let vertex_shader = load_shader("vertex_shader.spv");
    let fragment_shader = load_shader("fragment_shader.spv");

    // Initialize graphics pipeline and use shaders
    // More rendering setup and code goes here
}
```

In this code snippet, we load vertex and fragment shaders from separate files and prepare them for use in a graphics pipeline. The specifics of shader loading and compilation depend on the graphics API you are using and the libraries you choose.

2D and 3D Graphics

Rust provides libraries and frameworks for both 2D and 3D graphics. For 2D graphics, libraries like gfx2d and glium offer high-level abstractions for rendering sprites, textures, and simple shapes. These libraries simplify common 2D rendering tasks and can be a good choice for 2D game development.

For 3D graphics, more powerful engines like amethyst, bevy, or wgpu provide comprehensive solutions for handling 3D models, materials, lighting, and more. These engines often utilize modern graphics APIs like Vulkan or DirectX to deliver high-performance 3D rendering.

When working with graphics programming in Rust, it's crucial to choose the right libraries or frameworks based on your project's requirements and your familiarity with the tools. Graphics programming can be challenging, but Rust's safety features and active community support make it a viable choice for developing visually appealing and performant applications.

Section 13.4: Handling User Input and Events

User input and event handling are essential aspects of game development and interactive applications. In this section, we will explore how Rust handles user input and events, allowing developers to create responsive and interactive software.

Event Loop and Event Handling

Rust provides various libraries and frameworks for creating event-driven applications. Most game engines and graphical libraries have built-in event loops that handle input events like keyboard presses, mouse movements, and controller inputs.

For example, in the winit library, which is commonly used for creating windowed applications and games in Rust, you can set up an event loop to handle user input:

```rust
use winit::{
    event::{Event, WindowEvent},
    event_loop::{ControlFlow, EventLoop},
    window::WindowBuilder,
};

fn main() {
    let event_loop = EventLoop::new();
    let window = WindowBuilder::new().build(&event_loop).unwrap();

    event_loop.run(move |event, _, control_flow| {
        *control_flow = ControlFlow::Poll;
```

```rust
    match event {
        Event::WindowEvent {
            event: WindowEvent::CloseRequested,
            ..
        } => *control_flow = ControlFlow::Exit,
        Event::WindowEvent {
            event: WindowEvent::KeyboardInput { input, .. },
            ..
        } => {
            // Handle keyboard input
            if input.state == winit::event::ElementState::Pressed {
                match input.virtual_keycode {
                    Some(key) => match key {
                        winit::event::VirtualKeyCode::Escape => *control_
flow = ControlFlow::Exit,
                        _ => {}
                    },
                    None => {}
                }
            }
        }
        // Handle other input events here
        _ => {}
    }
});
}
```

In this example, we create a window using winit and set up an event loop to handle various events, including window close requests and keyboard input. You can customize event handling based on your application's requirements.

Input Handling Abstractions

Handling user input often involves managing keyboard, mouse, and controller inputs. Rust provides libraries like gilrs and sdl2 that offer high-level abstractions for input handling, making it easier to work with various input devices.

For instance, the gilrs library simplifies gamepad input handling:

```rust
use gilrs::{Gilrs, Button, Event, EventType};

fn main() {
    let mut gilrs = Gilrs::new().unwrap();

    loop {
        while let Some(Event { id, event, time, .. }) = gilrs.next_event() {
            match event {
                EventType::ButtonPressed(Button::South, _) => {
                    println!("Button South (A) pressed on gamepad {}", id);
                }
```

```
            EventType::ButtonReleased(Button::South, _) => {
                println!("Button South (A) released on gamepad {}", id);
            }
            // Handle other input events here
            _ => {}
        }
    }
}
```

In this code snippet, we use gilrs to handle gamepad input events, detecting when the "A" button is pressed or released. Similar abstractions exist for handling keyboard and mouse input with other libraries.

GUI Libraries

Graphical user interfaces (GUIs) often require handling user input for buttons, text fields, and other UI elements. Rust has several GUI libraries like druid, gtk-rs, and imgui-rs that provide tools for creating interactive GUI applications.

```
use druid::{AppLauncher, LocalizedString, PlatformError, Widget, WidgetExt, WindowDesc};

fn main() -> Result<(), PlatformError> {
    let main_window = WindowDesc::new(ui_builder);

    AppLauncher::with_window(main_window)
        .use_simple_logger()
        .launch("Hello, Druid!")?;

    Ok(())
}

fn ui_builder() -> impl Widget<()> {
    druid::TextBox::new().with_placeholder(LocalizedString::new("Enter your name"))
}
```

In this example, we use the druid library to create a simple text input field in a window. GUI libraries handle user input for GUI elements, allowing developers to create applications with interactive user interfaces.

Handling user input and events is a crucial part of building interactive applications and games in Rust. The choice of libraries and frameworks depends on your specific needs, whether you are developing games, graphical applications, or graphical user interfaces. Rust's ecosystem provides a range of options to suit different use cases.

Section 13.5: Building a Simple Game in Rust

Creating games in Rust has become increasingly popular due to its performance, safety features, and growing ecosystem of game development libraries and frameworks. In this section, we'll explore how to build a simple game in Rust, providing an overview of the essential components and libraries you can use.

Game Development Libraries

Before diving into game development, it's essential to choose the right libraries and frameworks that suit your game's requirements. Some popular options for game development in Rust include:

- **Amethyst:** A data-driven game engine that offers a powerful and extensible framework for building games. It provides tools for handling graphics, physics, and user input.

- **ggez:** A lightweight and easy-to-use 2D game framework for Rust. It abstracts away much of the low-level details, making it suitable for beginners.

- **piston:** A game engine framework that focuses on providing a simple and modular structure for game development. It offers various libraries for graphics, windowing, and input.

For our simple game example, we'll use the ggez framework to create a basic game loop and render graphics.

Setting Up the Project

To get started, you'll need to create a new Rust project and add the ggez crate as a dependency in your Cargo.toml file:

```
[dependencies]
ggez = "0.6"
```

Now, you can start writing your game code.

Creating a Game Loop

Every game needs a game loop to handle updates and rendering. In ggez, the game loop is provided through the EventHandler trait. Here's a minimal example of a game loop:

```
use ggez::{event, Context, GameResult};

struct MainState;

impl event::EventHandler for MainState {
    fn update(&mut self, _ctx: &mut Context) -> GameResult {
        // Update game logic here
        Ok(())
```

```
        }

    fn draw(&mut self, _ctx: &mut Context) -> GameResult {
        // Draw game elements here
        Ok(())
    }
}

fn main() -> GameResult {
    let (ctx, event_loop) = ggez::ContextBuilder::new("simple_game", "author"
)
        .build()?;
    let state = MainState;
    event::run(ctx, event_loop, state)
}
```

In this code, we define a `MainState` struct that implements the `EventHandler` trait from
ggez. The `update` function is called to update the game logic, and the `draw` function is called
to render the game elements. The `main` function sets up the game context and runs the
event loop.

Adding Game Logic and Graphics

To build a simple game, you can add game logic and graphics rendering within the `update`
and `draw` functions. For example, you can create a player character and move it around
using keyboard input.

```
use ggez::{event, Context, GameResult};
use ggez::graphics::{self, Rect};

struct MainState {
    player_x: f32,
    player_y: f32,
}

impl MainState {
    fn new() -> Self {
        MainState {
            player_x: 100.0,
            player_y: 100.0,
        }
    }
}

impl event::EventHandler for MainState {
    fn update(&mut self, _ctx: &mut Context) -> GameResult {
        // Update game logic here (e.g., move the player)
        Ok(())
    }
```

```rust
fn draw(&mut self, ctx: &mut Context) -> GameResult {
    graphics::clear(ctx, graphics::WHITE);

    // Draw game elements here (e.g., player character)
    let player_rect = Rect::new(self.player_x, self.player_y, 30.0, 30.0);

    let player_color = graphics::Color::new(0.0, 0.0, 1.0, 1.0);
    let player_mesh = graphics::Mesh::new_rectangle(ctx, graphics::DrawMode::fill(), player_rect, player_color)?;
    graphics::draw(ctx, &player_mesh, graphics::DrawParam::default())?;

    graphics::present(ctx)?;

    Ok(())
}
}

fn main() -> GameResult {
    let (ctx, event_loop) = ggez::ContextBuilder::new("simple_game", "author")
        .build()?;
    let state = MainState::new();
    event::run(ctx, event_loop, state)
}
```

In this updated code, we've added a player character represented as a colored rectangle. The update function can be used to handle player input and update the character's position. The draw function renders the player character on the screen.

Conclusion

This is a minimal example of building a simple game in Rust using the ggez framework. Game development in Rust offers various libraries and frameworks that cater to different needs and complexity levels. As you explore further, you can implement more advanced game features, add sprites, incorporate physics, and create interactive gameplay. Rust's performance and safety make it an excellent choice for both hobbyist and

Chapter 14: Rust and Cryptography

Section 14.1: Cryptographic Concepts in Rust

Cryptography is a crucial field in computer science that deals with secure communication, data integrity, and confidentiality. In this section, we will explore the fundamental cryptographic concepts and how Rust, with its focus on safety and performance, is well-suited for cryptographic applications.

What is Cryptography?

Cryptography is the practice of securing information by transforming it into an unreadable format, which can only be deciphered by someone with the proper key. It plays a vital role in ensuring data privacy, authentication, and secure communication over the internet.

Cryptographic Primitives

1. Hash Functions

Hash functions are mathematical functions that take an input (or 'message') and return a fixed-size string of bytes. The output, known as the hash value or digest, appears random and is unique to the input data. Commonly used hash functions in Rust include SHA-256, SHA-3, and Blake2.

Example (using the sha2 crate):

```rust
extern crate sha2;

use sha2::{Sha256, Digest};

fn main() {
    let mut hasher = Sha256::new();
    hasher.update(b"Hello, world!");
    let result = hasher.finalize();
    println!("{:x}", result);
}
```

2. Symmetric Encryption

Symmetric encryption algorithms use the same key for both encryption and decryption. Data encrypted with a specific key can only be decrypted with that same key. Rust provides libraries like rust-crypto and ring for symmetric encryption.

Example (using the rust-crypto crate):

```rust
extern crate crypto;

use crypto::symmetriccipher::SynchronousStreamCipher;
use crypto::aes::KeySize::KeySize256;
```

```rust
use crypto::aes::ecb_decryptor;

fn main() {
    let key = b"supersecretkey"; // 16-byte key
    let ciphertext = &[0u8; 16]; // Example ciphertext

    let mut decryptor = ecb_decryptor(KeySize256, key, crypto::blockmodes::No
Padding);
    let mut plaintext = vec![0; ciphertext.len()];
    decryptor.decrypt(ciphertext, &mut plaintext).unwrap();

    println!("{:?}", plaintext);
}
```

3. Asymmetric Encryption (Public Key Cryptography)

Asymmetric encryption uses a pair of keys: a public key for encryption and a private key for decryption. Data encrypted with the public key can only be decrypted with the corresponding private key. Libraries like openssl and rustls provide support for asymmetric encryption in Rust.

Example (using the openssl crate):

```rust
extern crate openssl;

use openssl::rsa::{Rsa, Padding};

fn main() {
    let rsa = Rsa::generate(2048).unwrap();
    let message = b"Hello, RSA!";

    let mut ciphertext = vec![0; rsa.size() as usize];
    rsa.public_encrypt(message, &mut ciphertext, Padding::PKCS1).unwrap();

    let mut plaintext = vec![0; rsa.size() as usize];
    rsa.private_decrypt(&ciphertext, &mut plaintext, Padding::PKCS1).unwrap()
;

    println!("{:?}", plaintext);
}
```

Conclusion

Understanding cryptographic concepts and implementing them securely is essential for building applications that require data security and privacy. Rust's focus on memory safety and performance makes it a robust choice for developing cryptographic applications, and its growing ecosystem of libraries provides developers with the tools they need to implement cryptographic primitives effectively. Whether you're securing communication, verifying data integrity, or implementing digital signatures, Rust can be a trusted companion in your cryptographic journey.

Section 14.2: Implementing Encryption Algorithms in Rust

In this section, we'll delve into the practical aspect of implementing encryption algorithms in Rust. Cryptographic algorithms are at the core of secure communication, and Rust's focus on safety and performance makes it an excellent choice for such implementations.

Choosing the Right Algorithm

Before implementing encryption in Rust, it's crucial to choose the appropriate cryptographic algorithm for your specific use case. The choice depends on factors like security requirements, performance, and the type of data you need to protect. Some common encryption algorithms include Advanced Encryption Standard (AES), RSA, and Elliptic Curve Cryptography (ECC).

Using External Libraries

While you can implement cryptographic algorithms from scratch in Rust, it's often more practical to leverage existing libraries that have been thoroughly reviewed and tested for security. Rust has a rich ecosystem of cryptographic libraries, such as rust-crypto, ring, and openssl, which provide high-quality implementations of various encryption algorithms.

Example of using the ring crate for AES encryption:

```rust
extern crate ring;

use ring::aead::{Aes256Gcm, UnboundKey, AES_256_GCM};
use ring::rand::SystemRandom;

fn main() {
    let rng = SystemRandom::new();
    let mut key_bytes = [0u8; 32]; // 256-bit AES key
    rng.fill(&mut key_bytes).unwrap();

    let unbound_key = UnboundKey::new(&AES_256_GCM, &key_bytes).unwrap();

    // Encrypt
    let nonce_bytes = [0u8; 12]; // 96-bit nonce
    let plaintext = b"Hello, AES!";
    let mut ciphertext = Vec::with_capacity(plaintext.len() + 16); // Allocat
e space for ciphertext and tag
    ciphertext.extend_from_slice(plaintext);
    Aes256Gcm.seal_in_place_append_tag(nonce_bytes, Default::default(), &unbo
```

```
und_key, &mut ciphertext).unwrap();

    // Decrypt
    let opened_data = Aes256Gcm.open_in_place(nonce_bytes, Default::default()
, &unbound_key, &mut ciphertext).unwrap();
    println!("{:?}", opened_data);
}
```

Implementing Custom Algorithms

In some cases, you may need to implement custom encryption algorithms tailored to your specific requirements. While this is a complex task that requires a deep understanding of cryptography and Rust's safety guarantees, it can be achieved safely in Rust.

For custom encryption implementations, Rust provides features like byte manipulation, low-level memory control, and safe abstractions to facilitate the development of secure cryptographic algorithms.

Secure Key Management

One of the most critical aspects of encryption is secure key management. Insecure key storage or transmission can compromise the entire encryption process. Rust's strong type system and memory safety features can help ensure that encryption keys are handled securely within your application.

When working with encryption in Rust, always follow best practices for key generation, storage, and transmission to maintain the security of your application.

Conclusion

Implementing encryption algorithms in Rust combines the language's safety features with the robustness of cryptographic libraries to create secure and efficient solutions. Whether you're using established libraries for common encryption tasks or developing custom algorithms for unique use cases, Rust provides the tools and safety guarantees required for cryptographic implementations. Remember to stay informed about the latest developments in cryptography and best practices to ensure the security of your applications.

Section 14.3: Rust in Blockchain and Cryptocurrency

In this section, we will explore how Rust is making significant inroads into the world of blockchain and cryptocurrency development. Rust's combination of performance, safety, and a strong type system makes it an ideal choice for building secure and efficient blockchain applications.

Building Blockchain Protocols

Blockchain technology relies on a decentralized, tamper-proof ledger of transactions. Rust's emphasis on memory safety and low-level control makes it well-suited for implementing blockchain protocols like Bitcoin, Ethereum, and others. Several blockchain projects have adopted Rust as their primary programming language for core development.

The `parity` project, for instance, is a Rust-based Ethereum client known for its high performance and reliability. Rust's strong type system helps reduce the risk of critical vulnerabilities in blockchain protocols, ensuring the security and stability of the network.

Smart Contracts and dApps

Smart contracts are self-executing contracts with the terms of the agreement directly written into code. They power decentralized applications (dApps) on blockchain platforms like Ethereum. Rust is gaining popularity as a language for writing smart contracts due to its safety features and performance advantages.

Projects like `ink!` provide Rust developers with a framework for creating Ethereum-compatible smart contracts. These contracts can be seamlessly integrated into the Ethereum ecosystem while benefiting from Rust's safety guarantees.

Cryptocurrency Wallets and Tools

Developing cryptocurrency wallets and tools requires a deep understanding of cryptographic principles and a focus on security. Rust's ability to write low-level code with memory safety ensures that cryptocurrency wallets and related software are resistant to common vulnerabilities, including buffer overflows and data leaks.

Wallet libraries like `bitcoin`, `rust-wallet`, and `elrond-wallet` have embraced Rust to provide users with secure and efficient cryptocurrency management tools.

Security Auditing and Penetration Testing

Rust's memory safety features are also valuable for security auditing and penetration testing of blockchain and cryptocurrency systems. Security researchers can use Rust to build custom tools for vulnerability discovery and analysis, helping to improve the overall security of blockchain networks.

Conclusion

Rust's adoption in the blockchain and cryptocurrency space continues to grow, driven by its ability to offer a balance between performance and safety. Whether you are building blockchain protocols, smart contracts, wallets, or conducting security audits, Rust provides the necessary tools and safety guarantees to create robust and secure solutions in this rapidly evolving field. As the blockchain ecosystem expands, Rust's role in shaping its future remains significant, promising a secure and efficient blockchain landscape.

Section 14.4: Secure Communication with Rust

In this section, we will explore how Rust plays a crucial role in ensuring secure communication in various software applications, including web servers, networking protocols, and messaging systems. Rust's emphasis on memory safety and zero-cost abstractions makes it well-suited for building secure communication tools.

Web Servers

Web servers are a common target for cyberattacks. Rust's memory safety guarantees help prevent common vulnerabilities like buffer overflows, null pointer dereferences, and data races, which are often exploited in web server attacks. The `actix-web` and `rocket` frameworks, both written in Rust, provide developers with robust tools for building high-performance, secure web servers.

Networking Protocols

Networking protocols form the backbone of communication on the internet. Rust's low-level control and strong type system make it an excellent choice for implementing and maintaining networking protocols. Libraries like `tokio` and `hyper` empower developers to create efficient, non-blocking network applications that are resistant to common security threats.

Messaging Systems

Messaging systems, including chat applications, email clients, and instant messaging platforms, rely on secure communication to protect user data. Rust's memory safety features help developers build messaging systems that are resilient to buffer overflows and other memory-related vulnerabilities.

Encryption and Authentication

Rust's cryptography libraries, such as `rustls` and `ring`, offer robust support for encryption and authentication. These libraries are essential for securing communication channels by providing secure transport layer protocols (TLS/SSL) and cryptographic primitives. Rust's memory safety ensures that cryptographic operations are protected from memory-related vulnerabilities, making it a reliable choice for secure communication.

Secure Coding Practices

Rust encourages secure coding practices through its type system and ownership model. Developers are less likely to introduce security vulnerabilities, such as SQL injection or cross-site scripting (XSS), when writing code in Rust. Rust's compiler catches many common security issues at compile-time, reducing the need for manual code reviews and audits.

Conclusion

Rust's focus on memory safety, performance, and a strong type system makes it a compelling choice for building secure communication systems. Whether you are developing web servers, networking protocols, messaging systems, or implementing encryption and authentication, Rust provides the tools and guarantees necessary to protect sensitive data and ensure secure communication channels. By adopting Rust, developers can reduce the risk of security breaches and strengthen the overall security posture of their applications and services.

Section 14.5: Building Cryptographically Secure Applications

In this concluding section of Chapter 14, we will discuss the importance of building cryptographically secure applications using Rust. Cryptography is a fundamental aspect of modern software development, as it helps protect sensitive data, secure communication channels, and ensure the integrity of information. Rust's focus on memory safety and its strong type system make it an ideal choice for developing cryptographically secure applications.

Why Cryptographic Security Matters

Cryptographic security is essential for various applications, including data protection, authentication, digital signatures, and secure communication. In an era of increasing cyber threats and data breaches, ensuring the confidentiality and integrity of data has become paramount. Cryptographic techniques, such as encryption, hashing, and digital signatures, play a crucial role in achieving these goals.

Rust's Role in Cryptographic Security

Rust provides several advantages when it comes to cryptographic security:

1. **Memory Safety**: Rust's ownership system and strict borrowing rules make it highly resilient to memory-related vulnerabilities. This is crucial in cryptographic applications, as memory safety prevents many common attack vectors like buffer overflows.

2. **Cryptography Libraries**: Rust has a thriving ecosystem of cryptographic libraries, such as ring, rust-crypto, and libsodium. These libraries offer robust implementations of cryptographic algorithms and protocols, ensuring that developers can rely on well-vetted code for secure operations.

3. **Static Analysis**: Rust's compiler performs static analysis to catch many potential issues at compile-time. This includes detecting unsafe code and ensuring that cryptographic operations are carried out correctly, reducing the risk of implementation errors.

Developers building cryptographically secure applications in Rust should follow best practices, including:

- **Using Well-Established Libraries**: Leverage established cryptographic libraries like `ring` or `rust-crypto` to implement cryptographic functionality. These libraries are continuously reviewed and updated to address emerging threats.

- **Key Management**: Properly manage cryptographic keys and ensure secure key storage. Rust's memory safety helps protect keys from being exposed or leaked in memory.

- **Secure Communication**: Implement secure communication protocols, such as TLS/SSL, to encrypt data in transit. Rust's libraries like `rustls` offer reliable TLS support.

- **Testing and Auditing**: Thoroughly test cryptographic code and consider external security audits. Rust's static analysis can help identify potential issues, but external validation is essential for security-critical applications.

- **Stay Informed**: Keep up-to-date with the latest developments in cryptography and security best practices. The field is constantly evolving, and staying informed is crucial for maintaining the security of your applications.

Conclusion

Building cryptographically secure applications is a critical aspect of software development, especially in an environment where data breaches and cyberattacks are prevalent. Rust's focus on memory safety, cryptographic libraries, and static analysis tools make it a strong choice for developers who prioritize security. By following best practices and leveraging Rust's capabilities, developers can create applications that protect sensitive data and communications from potential threats, contributing to a safer digital world.

Chapter 15: Rust for Data Science and Machine Learning

Section 15.1: Rust in the World of Data Science

In recent years, Rust has gained attention in the field of data science and machine learning, traditionally dominated by languages like Python and R. While Python is known for its ease of use and vast ecosystem of data science libraries, Rust offers its unique advantages that make it a compelling choice for certain data-intensive tasks.

The Advantages of Using Rust in Data Science

1. **Performance**: Rust is renowned for its performance and low-level control over system resources. In data science, where processing large datasets and running complex algorithms can be computationally intensive, Rust's speed can be a game-changer. Rust's memory safety ensures that you can achieve high performance without sacrificing safety.

2. **Concurrency**: Rust's ownership system allows for safe concurrent programming. This is crucial in data science, where parallelizing operations like data preprocessing or model training can significantly speed up tasks. Rust's concurrency features help you harness the full potential of multi-core processors.

3. **Embeddable**: Rust can be easily embedded within other languages like Python or C/C++. This means you can write performance-critical components in Rust while retaining the high-level scripting capabilities of Python, making Rust a versatile tool for data science projects.

4. **Safety**: Data integrity and security are paramount in data science, especially when dealing with sensitive data. Rust's memory safety features and static analysis can help catch potential issues at compile-time, reducing the risk of data corruption or security breaches.

5. **Community Efforts**: While Rust's data science ecosystem is not as mature as Python's, there are ongoing efforts to develop libraries and tools for data manipulation, numerical computing, and machine learning in Rust. Projects like ndarray, nalgebra, and tangram are examples of Rust's growing presence in this domain.

Use Cases for Rust in Data Science

Rust can be particularly beneficial in the following data science scenarios:

- **High-Performance Computing**: When you need to perform computationally intensive tasks, such as numerical simulations or scientific computing, Rust's speed and memory safety can be advantageous.

- **Data Preprocessing**: Rust can excel in data preprocessing tasks, where data is cleaned, transformed, and prepared for analysis. Its concurrency support can make these tasks more efficient.

- **Machine Learning Model Serving**: Rust is well-suited for serving machine learning models in production due to its performance and safety features.

- **Integration with Other Languages**: Rust can act as a bridge between high-level scripting languages like Python and lower-level languages like C/C++. This can be useful for implementing specific algorithms or components in Rust while leveraging existing libraries in Python.

Challenges and Considerations

While Rust offers many advantages for data science, it's essential to consider the following challenges:

- **Ecosystem Maturity**: Rust's data science ecosystem is still evolving, and it may not have the same breadth of libraries and tools as Python. You may need to develop certain functionalities yourself or integrate with libraries from other languages.

- **Learning Curve**: Rust has a steeper learning curve compared to languages like Python. Data scientists and machine learning practitioners may need some time to become proficient in Rust's syntax and ownership system.

- **Interoperability**: While Rust can be embedded in other languages, ensuring smooth interoperability can require careful design and integration efforts.

Conclusion

Rust's emergence in the field of data science and machine learning offers exciting opportunities for developers and data scientists. Its performance, safety, and concurrency features make it a valuable addition to the toolkit for tasks that demand high performance and data integrity. While Rust's ecosystem is still evolving, its unique strengths make it a compelling choice for specific data science use cases, complementing existing languages and tools in this domain.

Section 15.2: Data Processing and Analysis in Rust

Data processing and analysis are fundamental steps in any data science workflow. Rust, with its focus on performance, safety, and concurrency, can be a valuable choice for these tasks, especially when dealing with large datasets or computationally intensive operations.

Reading and Parsing Data

When working with data, the first step is often reading and parsing it. Rust provides libraries like csv, serde, and nom that make it easy to read and manipulate data in various formats, such as CSV, JSON, or binary. Here's a basic example of reading a CSV file using the csv crate:

```rust
use csv::ReaderBuilder;

fn main() -> Result<(), csv::Error> {
    let file = std::fs::File::open("data.csv")?;
    let mut rdr = ReaderBuilder::new().from_reader(file);

    for result in rdr.records() {
        let record = result?;
        // Process each record as needed
        println!("{:?}", record);
    }

    Ok(())
}
```

Data Transformation and Cleaning

Data is often messy and requires cleaning and transformation. Rust's expressive syntax and pattern matching can help you write clean and efficient code for these tasks. For example, you can use pattern matching to filter and transform data:

```rust
struct Person {
    name: String,
    age: u32,
}

fn main() {
    let people = vec![
        Person {
            name: "Alice".to_string(),
            age: 25,
        },
        Person {
            name: "Bob".to_string(),
            age: 30,
        },
        // More data...
    ];

    let adults: Vec<Person> = people
        .into_iter()
        .filter(|person| person.age >= 18)
        .collect();
```

```rust
    // 'adults' now contains only adult individuals
}
```

Numerical Computing

For numerical computations, Rust offers libraries like ndarray and nalgebra. These libraries provide support for multi-dimensional arrays, linear algebra operations, and numerical analysis. Here's an example of performing matrix multiplication using nalgebra:

```rust
use nalgebra::{Matrix2, Vector2};

fn main() {
    let a = Matrix2::new(1.0, 2.0, 3.0, 4.0);
    let b = Vector2::new(5.0, 6.0);

    let result = a * b;
    println!("{:?}", result);
}
```

Concurrency for Data Processing

Rust's ownership and concurrency model makes it well-suited for parallelizing data processing tasks. You can easily distribute data processing across multiple threads or even across multiple machines in a distributed computing environment. This can significantly speed up data analysis tasks, especially when dealing with large datasets.

```rust
use std::thread;

fn main() {
    let data = vec![1, 2, 3, 4, 5, 6, 7, 8, 9, 10];
    let num_threads = 4;

    let chunk_size = data.len() / num_threads;

    let handles: Vec<_> = (0..num_threads)
        .map(|i| {
            let start = i * chunk_size;
            let end = if i == num_threads - 1 {
                data.len()
            } else {
                (i + 1) * chunk_size
            };

            let chunk = &data[start..end];

            thread::spawn(move || {
                let sum: i32 = chunk.iter().sum();
                println!("Thread {}: Sum = {}", i, sum);
            })
```

```
    })
    .collect();

    for handle in handles {
        handle.join().unwrap();
    }
}
```

Visualization and Plotting

Data scientists often need to visualize results. While Rust's ecosystem for data visualization is not as extensive as that of Python, libraries like plotters and integration with Python's matplotlib can be used to create charts, plots, and graphs for data analysis.

In this section, we've explored how Rust can be used for data processing and analysis. Its performance, safety, and concurrency features make it a compelling choice for tasks that involve reading, cleaning, transforming, and analyzing data, especially in scenarios where performance is crucial. Rust's growing ecosystem of data science libraries and tools, coupled with its integration capabilities, make it a language to consider for data scientists and analysts.

Section 15.3: Machine Learning Libraries in Rust

Machine learning (ML) is a rapidly growing field that involves the development of algorithms and models to make predictions or decisions based on data. Rust is gaining traction as a language suitable for machine learning due to its performance, safety, and ecosystem of libraries tailored for numerical computation and ML. In this section, we will explore some of the ML libraries available in Rust.

1. ndarray and nalgebra

While not strictly ML libraries, ndarray and nalgebra are essential for ML tasks that involve numerical computations. ndarray provides support for multi-dimensional arrays, making it suitable for handling data, while nalgebra offers linear algebra operations necessary for many ML algorithms. These libraries form the foundation for building more specialized ML tools.

2. tangram

Tangram is an ML framework designed for simplicity and ease of use. It focuses on binary classification problems, making it ideal for tasks like fraud detection, churn prediction, or spam filtering. Tangram provides high-level abstractions and a user-friendly API for training and deploying models.

Here's a basic example of using Tangram to train a binary classifier:

```rust
use tangram_churn::ChurnModel;

fn main() {
    // Load your dataset
    let dataset = tangram::load_csv("churn.csv").unwrap();

    // Create a ChurnModel
    let mut model = ChurnModel::new();

    // Train the model
    model.train(dataset);

    // Make predictions
    let predictions = model.predict(dataset);

    // Evaluate the model
    let accuracy = model.evaluate(dataset);
    println!("Accuracy: {:.2}", accuracy);
}
```

3. rust-learn

Rust-Learn is a machine learning library for Rust that provides implementations of various ML algorithms. It includes support for regression, classification, clustering, and more. Rust-Learn is designed to be both efficient and easy to use.

Here's an example of using Rust-Learn for linear regression:

```rust
extern crate rustlearn;
extern crate rustlearn_toolbox;

use rustlearn::prelude::*;
use rustlearn::linear_model::SGDRegressor;

fn main() {
    // Load your dataset
    let (x, y) = load_your_data();

    // Create an SGDRegressor model
    let mut model = SGDRegressor::default();

    // Train the model
    model.fit(&x, &y);

    // Make predictions
    let predictions = model.predict(&x);

    // Evaluate the model
    let mse = mean_squared_error(&y, &predictions);
```

```
    println!("Mean Squared Error: {:.2}", mse);
}
```

4. tract

Tract is a TensorFlow-compatible neural network inference framework written in Rust. It allows you to run TensorFlow models efficiently, making it suitable for ML tasks involving deep learning. Tract supports various neural network architectures and can be used for tasks like image classification, object detection, and natural language processing.

These are just a few examples of ML libraries available in Rust. The Rust ecosystem is continually evolving, and new libraries and tools for machine learning are being developed. Whether you are interested in traditional ML algorithms, deep learning, or specialized ML tasks, Rust provides a growing set of options to explore and leverage its strengths in your ML projects.

Section 15.4: Building Predictive Models with Rust

Building predictive models is a fundamental aspect of machine learning and data science. In this section, we will explore how Rust can be used to create predictive models, focusing on the key steps involved in the process.

1. Data Preparation

Before building any predictive model, it's crucial to start with data preparation. This step includes tasks such as data cleaning, feature selection, and feature engineering. Rust provides libraries like ndarray and nalgebra to handle data efficiently, making it suitable for preprocessing tasks. Additionally, Rust's strong type system can help ensure data integrity throughout the process.

2. Model Selection

Selecting an appropriate predictive model is essential. Rust offers several libraries that support various machine learning algorithms, ranging from simple linear regression to complex deep learning models. The choice of a model depends on the nature of the problem, the available data, and the desired outcome.

3. Training the Model

Training a predictive model involves using historical data to "teach" the model to make accurate predictions. Rust libraries like rust-learn and tangram provide APIs for training models efficiently. During this step, you'll typically split your data into training and testing sets to evaluate the model's performance.

4. Model Evaluation

Evaluating a predictive model helps assess its accuracy and reliability. Rust offers libraries for calculating various metrics like mean squared error (MSE), accuracy, precision, recall, and F1-score. These metrics help you understand how well your model is performing and whether it meets your project's requirements.

5. Hyperparameter Tuning

Hyperparameter tuning involves finding the best set of hyperparameters for your model to optimize its performance. Rust provides tools for grid search and random search to explore different hyperparameter combinations systematically.

6. Deployment

Once you have a trained and validated predictive model, you can deploy it to make real-time predictions or integrate it into your application. Rust's focus on performance and safety makes it a suitable choice for deploying machine learning models in production environments.

7. Monitoring and Maintenance

After deployment, it's crucial to monitor your predictive model's performance and retrain it periodically to adapt to changing data patterns. Rust's reliability and ease of maintenance ensure that your predictive models continue to provide accurate results over time.

Here's a simplified example of building a predictive model for linear regression in Rust using the rust-learn library:

```rust
extern crate rustlearn;
extern crate rustlearn_toolbox;

use rustlearn::prelude::*;
use rustlearn::linear_model::SGDRegressor;

fn main() {
    // Load your dataset
    let (x, y) = load_your_data();

    // Create an SGDRegressor model
    let mut model = SGDRegressor::default();

    // Train the model
    model.fit(&x, &y);

    // Make predictions
    let predictions = model.predict(&x);

    // Evaluate the model
    let mse = mean_squared_error(&y, &predictions);
```

```
    println!("Mean Squared Error: {:.2}", mse);
}
```

This example demonstrates the essential steps in building a predictive model using Rust. Keep in mind that the choice of libraries and algorithms may vary depending on your specific machine learning task, and the Rust ecosystem provides flexibility and scalability to meet your project's needs.

Section 15.5: Case Studies: Rust in Data Intensive Applications

In this section, we'll explore case studies where Rust has been successfully applied in data-intensive applications. Rust's performance, safety, and suitability for systems programming make it an excellent choice for handling large-scale data processing and analysis tasks.

1. Servo: A Modern Web Browser Engine

One notable example is Servo, a next-generation web browser engine developed by Mozilla. Servo is written primarily in Rust and aims to provide improved performance, security, and parallelism. Rust's memory safety guarantees are particularly valuable when processing complex web content, preventing common vulnerabilities like buffer overflows. Servo's parallel architecture leverages Rust's concurrency features to optimize web page rendering and loading.

2. Tantivy: A Full-Text Search Engine Library

Tantivy is an open-source full-text search engine library implemented in Rust. It is designed for efficiency and scalability, making it suitable for building search engines and information retrieval systems. Tantivy's performance is a result of Rust's memory management and multithreading capabilities. This library demonstrates how Rust can excel in data-intensive applications where low-level control is essential.

3. DataFusion: A Distributed SQL Query Engine

DataFusion is a modern distributed SQL query engine written in Rust. It provides fast query execution and supports multiple data sources. Rust's memory safety and zero-cost abstractions are crucial for building a reliable and high-performance query engine. DataFusion showcases Rust's ability to handle data-intensive workloads efficiently.

4. Parquet: A Columnar Storage Format

The Apache Parquet project, used for columnar storage, has a Rust implementation called "parquet-rs." Columnar storage is widely used in data analytics and data warehousing. The Rust implementation leverages memory safety to ensure data integrity and takes advantage of Rust's performance characteristics to achieve efficient compression and decompression of columnar data.

5. Heim: A Cross-Platform System Information Library

Heim is a cross-platform system information library written in Rust. It provides APIs for retrieving information about hardware and system resources, making it valuable for data-intensive applications that require system monitoring and resource management. Rust's portability and safety are essential for such low-level system interaction.

6. Polars: A Data Manipulation and Analysis Library

Polars is a fast DataFrame library for Rust and Python. It focuses on data manipulation, transformation, and analysis, making it a strong contender for data-intensive applications. Rust's memory safety and performance optimization are significant advantages for a library like Polars, enabling efficient data operations even on large datasets.

These case studies demonstrate the versatility and effectiveness of Rust in handling data-intensive applications across various domains, from web browsers to search engines and distributed query engines. Rust's features, including memory safety, concurrency, and performance, make it an appealing choice for data professionals and developers working on data-centric projects.

Chapter 16: Scalability and Performance in Rust

Section 16.1: Writing High-Performance Rust Code

In this section, we will explore various techniques for writing high-performance Rust code. Rust is known for its focus on both safety and performance, making it an excellent choice for applications where speed and efficiency are crucial.

Performance Considerations in Rust

Before diving into specific techniques, it's essential to understand the factors that influence performance in Rust.

1. **Ownership and Borrowing**: Rust's ownership system minimizes runtime overhead by ensuring memory safety at compile-time. By using ownership and borrowing correctly, you can avoid unnecessary memory allocations and deallocations, leading to improved performance.

2. **Concurrency and Parallelism**: Rust provides powerful abstractions for concurrent and parallel programming. Leveraging Rust's concurrency features can help you take full advantage of multi-core processors and distributed systems.

3. **Memory Management**: Managing memory efficiently is vital for performance. Rust's control over memory allocation and deallocation allows you to minimize memory fragmentation and overhead.

4. **Data Structures**: Choosing the right data structures can significantly impact performance. Rust's standard library provides efficient collections, but sometimes, custom data structures tailored to your application's needs can offer even better performance.

5. **Optimizations**: Rust's compiler, rustc, includes various optimization levels. Choosing the appropriate optimization level for your project can significantly improve runtime performance.

Profiling and Benchmarking

Before optimizing your Rust code, it's crucial to identify performance bottlenecks. Profiling tools, such as perf and flamegraph, can help you pinpoint areas of your code that need improvement. Additionally, Rust provides the cargo command-line tool with built-in support for benchmarking.

Writing Efficient Algorithms

Algorithmic efficiency plays a critical role in performance. Choosing the right algorithm and data structure for a given problem can lead to substantial speed improvements. Rust's expressive type system makes it easy to implement and experiment with different algorithms.

Memory Management and Optimization

Rust allows you fine-grained control over memory, but it also offers abstractions like smart pointers and reference counting for more convenient memory management. Understanding when and how to use these abstractions can lead to better memory efficiency.

Profiling Rust Code

Profiling your Rust code is essential to identify bottlenecks and areas for improvement. Rust provides tools like `perf`, `flamegraph`, and `cargo` profilers to help you gain insights into your program's runtime behavior.

SIMD (Single Instruction, Multiple Data)

Rust has support for SIMD operations, allowing you to take advantage of vectorized processing units like SSE and AVX. SIMD can significantly boost performance in compute-intensive applications, such as image processing and numerical simulations.

Parallelism and Concurrency

Rust's ownership system and the `std::sync` module enable safe and efficient parallel and concurrent programming. Utilizing multiple threads or asynchronous tasks can lead to improved throughput and reduced latency in your applications.

Load Balancing and High Availability

In distributed systems, load balancing and high availability are crucial for maintaining optimal performance and reliability. Rust provides libraries and frameworks for building scalable and fault-tolerant applications.

Real-World Case Studies

To illustrate these performance techniques in action, we will examine real-world case studies of Rust projects that have achieved exceptional performance gains using various optimization strategies.

In the following sections, we will delve deeper into each of these topics, providing practical examples and code snippets to help you write high-performance Rust code for your applications.

Section 16.2: Memory Management and Optimization

Efficient memory management is a crucial aspect of writing high-performance Rust code. Rust's ownership system and strict memory safety guarantees help prevent common memory-related issues, but it's essential to optimize memory usage for better performance.

Stack vs. Heap

Rust encourages using the stack for small, short-lived variables and the heap for dynamic data with a longer lifetime. Stack allocation is generally faster than heap allocation because it involves only adjusting the stack pointer, while heap allocation requires interacting with the memory allocator.

```rust
fn stack_vs_heap() {
    // Stack allocation
    let x = 42;  // Stored on the stack

    // Heap allocation
    let y = Box::new(42);  // Stored on the heap
}
```

Lifetimes and Borrowing

Understanding lifetimes and borrowing in Rust is essential for efficient memory management. By correctly annotating lifetimes and using borrowing and references, you can minimize unnecessary copying and allocation of data.

```rust
fn compute_length(s: &str) -> usize {
    s.len()
}

fn main() {
    let s1 = String::from("hello");
    let len = compute_length(&s1); // Pass a reference, not the whole String
}
```

Reusing Memory

Reusing memory whenever possible can significantly improve performance. Instead of repeatedly allocating and deallocating memory, consider using data structures that allow efficient resizing and reusing allocated memory, like Vec with the `with_capacity` method.

```rust
fn efficient_memory_reuse() {
    let mut vec = Vec::with_capacity(10); // Preallocate memory
    for i in 0..10 {
        vec.push(i);
    }
    // vec continues to use the allocated memory
}
```

Copy vs. Clone

Rust's Copy and Clone traits impact how values are duplicated. Types that implement Copy are duplicated implicitly on assignments, while those implementing Clone require explicit cloning.

```rust
#[derive(Copy, Clone)]
struct Point {
    x: i32,
    y: i32,
}

fn main() {
    let p1 = Point { x: 1, y: 2 };
    let p2 = p1; // p1 is copied because Point implements Copy
}
```

Rust's Allocator API

Rust provides an allocator API that allows custom memory allocators. You can use this to implement specialized allocators tailored to your application's needs, further optimizing memory management.

```rust
use std::alloc::{GlobalAlloc, System, Layout};

struct MyAllocator;

unsafe impl GlobalAlloc for MyAllocator {
    unsafe fn alloc(&self, layout: Layout) -> *mut u8 {
        System.alloc(layout)
    }

    unsafe fn dealloc(&self, ptr: *mut u8, layout: Layout) {
        System.dealloc(ptr, layout);
    }
}
```

Cache-Friendly Data Structures

Cache locality is critical for performance. Choosing data structures and memory layouts that are cache-friendly can reduce memory latency and improve CPU cache utilization.

In this section, we've explored memory management and optimization techniques in Rust. Efficient memory usage and management are key to achieving high-performance Rust code. By understanding the nuances of Rust's memory model, leveraging lifetimes and borrowing, and making informed choices about data structures, you can write code that not only runs safely but also performs exceptionally well.

Section 16.3: Scalable System Architectures

Scalability is a critical aspect of high-performance systems. It refers to a system's ability to handle increased workloads efficiently without sacrificing performance. In Rust, building scalable systems involves designing software architectures that can take advantage of modern hardware capabilities.

Parallelism and Concurrency

Rust excels at parallelism and concurrency, making it well-suited for building scalable systems. The std::thread module allows you to create threads for parallel execution, while the std::sync module provides synchronization primitives like mutexes and channels for communication between threads.

```rust
use std::thread;

fn main() {
    let handle = thread::spawn(|| {
        // Code to be executed in a separate thread
    });

    // Main thread continues its work

    handle.join().unwrap(); // Wait for the spawned thread to finish
}
```

Asynchronous Programming

Rust's async/await syntax, introduced in recent versions, enables asynchronous programming. It allows you to write non-blocking code that can efficiently handle many tasks concurrently. Asynchronous code is particularly valuable in I/O-bound operations.

```rust
use async_std::task;

async fn async_function() {
    // Asynchronous code
}

fn main() {
    let task = task::spawn(async_function());

    // Main thread continues its work

    task::block_on(task); // Wait for the asynchronous task to complete
}
```

Message Passing

Message passing is a fundamental concept in building scalable systems. Rust's channels, provided by the std::sync::mpsc module, allow threads to send and receive messages safely. This mechanism is useful for orchestrating work among multiple threads or processes.

```rust
use std::sync::mpsc;
use std::thread;

fn main() {
    let (tx, rx) = mpsc::channel();

    let producer = thread::spawn(move || {
        tx.send("Message from producer").unwrap();
    });

    let consumer = thread::spawn(move || {
        let received = rx.recv().unwrap();
        println!("Received: {}", received);
    });

    producer.join().unwrap();
    consumer.join().unwrap();
}
```

Load Balancing and High Availability

In scalable systems, distributing workloads and ensuring high availability are essential. Load balancing techniques, such as round-robin or weighted load balancing, can evenly distribute incoming requests across multiple server instances or threads. Additionally, redundancy and failover mechanisms ensure that the system remains available even in the face of failures.

Horizontal Scaling

Horizontal scaling involves adding more instances or nodes to a system to handle increased loads. Rust's support for concurrent and parallel programming makes it easier to scale applications horizontally by adding more threads or processes. Technologies like Kubernetes and Docker can assist in managing the deployment and scaling of Rust applications.

Microservices and Containerization

Microservices architecture divides a large system into smaller, independent services that can be developed, deployed, and scaled individually. Containerization technologies like Docker enable the packaging of microservices into lightweight, portable containers. Rust's small binary sizes and low resource requirements make it a good fit for microservices.

In this section, we've explored various aspects of building scalable system architectures in Rust. From parallelism and asynchronous programming to message passing and load balancing, Rust provides the tools and language features needed to create high-performance, scalable systems that can efficiently handle increasing workloads while maintaining reliability and responsiveness.

Section 16.4: Load Balancing and High Availability

Load balancing and high availability are essential concepts when building scalable and robust systems. In this section, we'll explore how Rust can be employed to implement effective load balancing and ensure high availability in distributed applications.

Load Balancing

Load balancing is the distribution of incoming network traffic or workload across multiple servers or resources. It ensures that no single server or resource is overwhelmed while others remain underutilized, thus optimizing resource usage and preventing system bottlenecks.

Rust can play a crucial role in load balancing through the development of load balancer components that efficiently distribute incoming requests or tasks. Let's consider a simple example using Rust to create a load balancer:

```rust
use std::net::{SocketAddr, TcpListener, TcpStream};
use std::thread;

fn handle_client(stream: TcpStream) {
    // Handle incoming client requests here
}

fn main() {
    let listener = TcpListener::bind("0.0.0.0:8080").expect("Failed to bind")
;

    for stream in listener.incoming() {
        match stream {
            Ok(stream) => {
                // Spawn a new thread to handle the client request
                thread::spawn(|| {
                    handle_client(stream);
                });
            }
            Err(e) => {
                eprintln!("Error: {}", e);
            }
        }
    }
}
```

In this example, a simple TCP-based load balancer is created. It listens for incoming client connections and delegates each connection to a separate thread for processing. This basic load balancing mechanism distributes client requests across multiple threads, improving system responsiveness.

High Availability

High availability refers to the ability of a system to remain operational and accessible even in the presence of failures. Rust's reliability and robustness make it a suitable choice for building high availability systems.

Achieving high availability often involves redundancy and failover mechanisms. Rust allows developers to implement these mechanisms effectively. For instance, using Rust's robust error handling, you can gracefully handle failures and switch to backup systems or nodes when needed.

```rust
use std::net::{TcpListener, TcpStream};
use std::thread;

fn main() {
    let listener = TcpListener::bind("0.0.0.0:8080").expect("Failed to bind");

    // Continuously listen for incoming connections
    for stream in listener.incoming() {
        match stream {
            Ok(stream) => {
                // Handle the client request in a new thread
                thread::spawn(|| {
                    handle_client(stream);
                });
            }
            Err(e) => {
                eprintln!("Error: {}", e);
                // Handle the error and initiate failover procedures
                // ...
            }
        }
    }
}

fn handle_client(stream: TcpStream) {
    // Handle the client request here
}
```

In this example, error handling is employed to manage unexpected issues. When an error occurs, the system can initiate failover procedures, such as redirecting requests to backup servers or notifying system administrators.

Distributed Systems and Rust

Distributed systems often rely on Rust due to its memory safety and performance advantages. Technologies like Apache Kafka, etcd, and others have Rust components that contribute to their overall reliability and scalability.

200

Rust's ability to handle concurrency and its support for low-level systems programming are well-suited for building distributed systems that require precise control over resource management and communication between nodes.

In summary, Rust can be a valuable tool for implementing load balancing and ensuring high availability in distributed applications. Its robust error handling, concurrency support, and memory safety make it an excellent choice for building scalable and reliable systems that can efficiently distribute workloads and handle failures gracefully.

Section 16.5: Case Studies: Performance Optimization in Rust

In this section, we'll delve into real-world case studies that showcase the effectiveness of Rust in performance optimization. Rust's focus on memory safety, zero-cost abstractions, and fine-grained control over resources makes it a powerful tool for achieving high-performance computing.

Case Study 1: Servo Browser Engine

One of the most prominent examples of Rust's performance capabilities is the Servo web browser engine, developed by Mozilla. Servo was designed from the ground up to harness the full power of modern hardware while maintaining security and reliability.

Rust's ownership system and fearless concurrency played a vital role in Servo's development. By eliminating data races and memory-related bugs at compile time, Rust ensured that Servo's codebase was robust and efficient. Servo's parallel layout engine leveraged Rust's concurrency features to achieve remarkable performance improvements in rendering web pages.

Case Study 2: Tokio Asynchronous Runtime

Tokio is an asynchronous runtime for Rust that enables developers to write asynchronous, non-blocking code. It's widely used in building high-performance network services, such as web servers and proxies.

Rust's ownership model and async/await syntax make it possible to write concurrent code that is both safe and performant. Tokio leverages these features to handle thousands of concurrent connections efficiently. It's a prime example of how Rust empowers developers to build high-performance, asynchronous systems.

Case Study 3: Data Serialization with Serde

Serde is a Rust library for data serialization and deserialization. It's used in numerous projects, including databases, web services, and data processing pipelines.

Serde's design takes advantage of Rust's zero-cost abstractions and efficient memory management. It provides a highly optimized and safe way to serialize and deserialize data structures. By using Rust's traits system and generics, Serde achieves performance that rivals hand-written serialization code while maintaining safety guarantees.

Case Study 4: Rust in Game Development

The game development industry demands high-performance code to deliver smooth and immersive gaming experiences. Rust is increasingly being adopted in this domain due to its ability to meet these requirements.

Game engines like Amethyst and game frameworks like ggez showcase Rust's prowess in game development. Rust's memory safety and performance optimizations allow game developers to create complex, resource-intensive games without sacrificing speed or reliability.

Case Study 5: Rust in Cryptocurrency

Cryptocurrency implementations require high performance and security due to the sensitive nature of financial transactions. Several blockchain projects, such as Solana and Polkadot, have chosen Rust for their core components.

Rust's safety features ensure that critical blockchain operations are free from vulnerabilities and exploits. Additionally, Rust's performance optimizations make it possible to process thousands of transactions per second while maintaining the security guarantees expected in the blockchain space.

In conclusion, Rust's emphasis on performance, safety, and control over system resources has led to its adoption in various domains where high-performance computing is crucial. These case studies demonstrate how Rust empowers developers to build efficient and reliable software across a wide range of applications, from web browsers to game engines and blockchain platforms.

Chapter 17: Rust in the Enterprise

Section 17.1: Adopting Rust in Large-Scale Projects

In this section, we'll explore the adoption of Rust in large-scale enterprise projects and discuss why many organizations are turning to Rust for their critical software development needs. Rust's unique combination of safety, performance, and productivity has made it an attractive choice for businesses tackling complex and mission-critical applications.

The Rust Safety Promise

One of the primary reasons for Rust's adoption in the enterprise is its focus on safety. Large-scale projects often involve extensive codebases with numerous developers contributing code over time. Ensuring the safety and reliability of such projects becomes increasingly challenging.

Rust's ownership system, borrow checker, and lifetime management help eliminate entire classes of bugs, such as null pointer dereferences and data races. By catching these issues at compile-time, Rust reduces the need for extensive testing and debugging, making it easier to develop and maintain large systems.

Performance at Scale

Enterprise applications often deal with high loads, requiring optimal performance. Rust's low-level control over system resources and the absence of a garbage collector contribute to predictable and efficient runtime performance. This is crucial for applications handling massive amounts of data or serving thousands of concurrent users.

Furthermore, Rust's ability to interface seamlessly with C and C++ libraries allows organizations to leverage existing codebases and libraries, reducing development time and costs.

Productivity and Maintainability

While Rust is known for its safety and performance, it also places a strong emphasis on developer productivity. The language's expressive syntax and rich ecosystem of libraries and tools enable developers to write clean and maintainable code.

Rust's package manager, Cargo, simplifies dependency management, ensuring that large projects remain organized and that dependencies are kept up-to-date. The extensive documentation and strong community support also contribute to a productive development environment.

Real-World Examples

Numerous enterprises, including Dropbox, AWS, and Microsoft, have adopted Rust for various projects. Dropbox, for instance, used Rust to optimize its file synchronization engine, resulting in significant performance improvements. AWS has incorporated Rust into its services for improved security and performance, particularly in resource-constrained environments.

These real-world success stories highlight the benefits of adopting Rust in enterprise settings. It offers a winning combination of safety, performance, and developer productivity, making it a valuable tool for organizations looking to build robust and scalable software solutions.

Overcoming Challenges

While Rust brings many advantages to enterprise development, adopting a new programming language can present challenges. These include the need to train existing teams, integrate Rust into existing tech stacks, and navigate the learning curve associated with Rust's unique features.

However, as Rust's popularity continues to grow and more resources become available, these challenges are becoming easier to overcome. The long-term benefits of adopting Rust often outweigh the initial hurdles, making it a compelling choice for enterprises aiming to build secure, high-performance software at scale.

In summary, Rust's safety, performance, and productivity advantages have led to its increasing adoption in the enterprise sector. Its ability to deliver robust, efficient, and maintainable solutions makes it an attractive choice for tackling complex projects, ensuring the continued growth of Rust's presence in the corporate world.

Section 17.2: Rust for Enterprise Security

In this section, we will delve into how Rust addresses security concerns and why it has become a popular choice for building secure enterprise applications. Security is paramount for businesses, especially when dealing with sensitive data and critical systems. Rust's design and features make it a compelling option for organizations aiming to fortify their software against security vulnerabilities.

Memory Safety and Security

Memory safety is a fundamental aspect of security in software development. Many security breaches, such as buffer overflows and memory corruption exploits, stem from memory-related vulnerabilities. Rust's ownership system and strict compile-time checks eliminate these vulnerabilities by design.

By preventing common memory errors at compile-time, Rust minimizes the attack surface for potential security threats. This means that security vulnerabilities related to memory manipulation are considerably less likely to occur in Rust codebases.

Protection Against Data Races

Data races, which can lead to unpredictable behavior and security vulnerabilities, are another common concern in concurrent programming. Rust's ownership and borrowing model, coupled with its robust concurrency guarantees, ensure that data races are virtually impossible to introduce into Rust code. This makes Rust an excellent choice for building highly concurrent systems that remain secure even under heavy loads.

Secure by Default

Rust follows a "secure by default" philosophy, which means that potentially unsafe operations require explicit annotation. The unsafe keyword is used to mark code blocks that bypass Rust's safety checks, and these blocks must be justified and reviewed carefully.

This approach ensures that unsafe operations are a conscious decision by the developer and are subjected to scrutiny. It also means that the majority of Rust code remains safe by design, reducing the likelihood of security vulnerabilities.

Third-Party Audits

Rust's security features and libraries are regularly audited by both the Rust community and external security experts. This transparent and community-driven approach helps identify and address potential security issues promptly.

Organizations adopting Rust can benefit from these audits, gaining confidence in the language's ability to provide secure solutions. Additionally, Rust's security-conscious ecosystem ensures that libraries and dependencies are actively maintained and updated to address emerging threats.

Cryptography and Secure Communication

Rust is well-suited for cryptographic and secure communication applications. It provides a range of libraries for implementing encryption algorithms, secure authentication, and secure transport protocols. These libraries are developed with security as a primary concern and are designed to resist attacks and vulnerabilities.

Furthermore, Rust's strong type system and ownership model make it easier to reason about security-critical code, reducing the potential for security oversights.

Secure Enterprise Solutions in Rust

Many enterprises, particularly those in sectors such as finance, healthcare, and government, have adopted Rust to build secure and mission-critical systems. Rust's emphasis on security, combined with its performance and developer productivity benefits, makes it an ideal choice for applications that demand the highest level of protection.

In conclusion, Rust's memory safety, data race prevention, secure-by-default approach, and security-conscious ecosystem position it as a powerful tool for enterprise security. Organizations seeking to fortify their software against security vulnerabilities can leverage Rust to build robust and resilient applications.

Section 17.3: Building Microservices with Rust

Microservices architecture has gained immense popularity in recent years due to its flexibility, scalability, and ease of maintenance. In this section, we will explore how Rust can be an excellent choice for building microservices, offering advantages like performance, safety, and productivity.

Performance and Efficiency

Microservices often require low-latency communication and efficient resource utilization. Rust's performance characteristics make it suitable for building high-throughput microservices that can handle a significant number of requests with minimal resource consumption.

Rust's zero-cost abstractions and fine-grained control over system resources allow developers to optimize their microservices for performance. This is crucial for applications that need to scale horizontally to accommodate a growing user base.

Safety and Reliability

The safety features of Rust are particularly valuable in a microservices context. Each microservice operates independently, often with its own set of data and interactions. Ensuring that each service is free from common programming errors and vulnerabilities is vital.

Rust's ownership system, memory safety guarantees, and compile-time checks reduce the risk of security vulnerabilities, crashes, and bugs in microservices. This translates to improved overall system reliability and a reduced likelihood of service interruptions.

Concurrency and Parallelism

Microservices often need to handle concurrent requests efficiently. Rust's concurrency model, which includes lightweight threads (known as "async/await"), ensures that microservices can be highly responsive and handle many concurrent connections with ease.

Rust's approach to concurrency minimizes the overhead of managing threads and ensures that the system remains efficient even under heavy loads. This is crucial for microservices that must scale horizontally to meet increased demand.

Ecosystem and Libraries

Rust boasts a growing ecosystem of libraries and frameworks for building microservices. Tools like Actix, Rocket, and Warp provide web frameworks that make it straightforward to create RESTful APIs and handle HTTP requests.

Additionally, Rust's support for asynchronous programming simplifies the development of non-blocking microservices that can efficiently utilize system resources. This allows for building responsive and highly scalable microservices.

Containerization and Deployment

Microservices are often deployed using containerization technologies like Docker and container orchestration platforms like Kubernetes. Rust seamlessly integrates with these technologies, making it easy to package microservices into containers and deploy them on various cloud providers or on-premises infrastructure.

Rust's small binary sizes and minimal runtime dependencies contribute to efficient containerization, reducing image sizes and startup times. This is advantageous when deploying and managing a large number of microservices.

Cross-Platform Compatibility

Microservices may run on diverse environments, including different operating systems and architectures. Rust's cross-platform compatibility ensures that microservices written in Rust can be deployed across a wide range of platforms without modification. This flexibility simplifies deployment and reduces potential compatibility issues.

In conclusion, Rust is well-suited for building microservices that require high performance, safety, and reliability. Its language features, concurrency model, ecosystem, and compatibility with containerization technologies make it a compelling choice for organizations looking to develop scalable and efficient microservices-based applications. By leveraging Rust, developers can create microservices that are both performant and secure, contributing to the success of their microservices architecture.

Section 17.4: Rust in Cloud Computing

Cloud computing has revolutionized the way organizations build, deploy, and manage their applications. Rust's characteristics make it a strong candidate for developing cloud-native applications and services. In this section, we'll explore how Rust fits into the cloud computing landscape.

Serverless Computing

Serverless computing platforms like AWS Lambda, Azure Functions, and Google Cloud Functions allow developers to run code without provisioning or managing servers. Rust's small binary sizes and low resource consumption make it an excellent choice for serverless applications. Developers can write efficient and cost-effective serverless functions in Rust.

Rust's support for writing AWS Lambda functions is facilitated by libraries like aws-lambda-rust-runtime, which simplify the integration of Rust code with AWS Lambda. This enables developers to leverage Rust's performance and safety benefits in serverless environments.

Containers and Orchestration

Containers have become a standard for packaging and deploying applications in the cloud. Rust's compatibility with containerization technologies like Docker enables developers to create lightweight and efficient container images. The Rust ecosystem offers tools and libraries to simplify containerized application development.

Container orchestration platforms like Kubernetes are widely used to manage containerized applications at scale. Rust developers can use tools like Krustlet, a Kubernetes kubelet written in Rust, to run Rust workloads seamlessly on Kubernetes clusters. This flexibility allows Rust applications to take full advantage of container orchestration and scaling capabilities.

Cloud-Native Databases

Rust's performance and safety characteristics extend to database development. Cloud-native databases often require high throughput and low-latency access to data. Rust's suitability for systems programming makes it a valuable choice for building databases tailored to cloud-native environments.

Rust database libraries like `sled` and `rust-postgres` enable developers to create cloud-native databases with excellent performance and data consistency. These libraries take advantage of Rust's concurrency and memory safety features, ensuring the reliability of cloud-native database solutions.

Cloud Infrastructure as Code

Infrastructure as code (IaC) is a practice that treats infrastructure provisioning and management as code. Rust can be used to create IaC scripts and tools that define and manage cloud infrastructure.

Developers can leverage Rust to write custom IaC solutions using cloud provider APIs. For example, Rust's support for AWS SDKs allows developers to automate the provisioning and management of AWS resources. This approach provides greater flexibility and control over cloud infrastructure configurations.

Cloud-Native Monitoring and Observability

Monitoring and observability are critical aspects of cloud-native applications. Rust can be used to build monitoring agents, telemetry collectors, and observability tools. Rust's low overhead and performance characteristics make it suitable for capturing and analyzing telemetry data in real-time.

By developing monitoring and observability components in Rust, organizations can ensure that their cloud-native applications are effectively monitored and debugged. Rust's safety guarantees also contribute to the reliability of these critical systems.

In summary, Rust's performance, safety, and compatibility with cloud technologies make it a compelling choice for developing cloud-native applications and services. Whether for serverless computing, container orchestration, databases, infrastructure automation, or observability, Rust's features align with the requirements of modern cloud computing environments. As organizations increasingly adopt cloud-native approaches, Rust is poised to play a significant role in shaping the future of cloud-native development.

Section 17.5: Case Studies: Rust in Corporate Environments

In this section, we will delve into real-world case studies of how Rust has been successfully employed within corporate environments. These case studies demonstrate the practicality and effectiveness of Rust in solving various challenges faced by organizations.

Dropbox: Rewriting Critical Components for Safety and Performance

Dropbox, a widely-used cloud storage and file-sharing service, faced challenges related to the performance and security of their storage system. To address these issues, Dropbox decided to rewrite critical components of their storage stack in Rust. They chose Rust for its memory safety guarantees and ability to deliver high-performance code.

By transitioning to Rust, Dropbox achieved significant improvements in both performance and security. Rust's ownership model eliminated common bugs related to memory management, resulting in more reliable software. Additionally, Rust's multi-threading capabilities allowed Dropbox to better utilize modern hardware, enhancing the overall performance of their storage infrastructure.

Mozilla: Building a More Secure Web Browser

Mozilla, the organization behind the Firefox web browser, has been actively using Rust to build components of their browser engine. They developed "Servo," a browser engine project written in Rust, with the aim of creating a more secure and parallelized engine. Servo's development highlighted Rust's suitability for writing system-level software with a focus on security and parallelism.

While Servo itself didn't replace the entire Firefox browser, it served as a valuable testing ground for new ideas and technologies. Some of Servo's innovations have made their way into Firefox, contributing to the overall security and performance of the browser.

Cloudflare: Leveraging Rust for Networking and Security

Cloudflare, a company providing cloud-based web performance and security services, embraced Rust to enhance their infrastructure. They found Rust particularly suitable for building networking and security-related tools and services.

One of Cloudflare's Rust projects is "quiche," an implementation of the QUIC transport protocol. QUIC is designed for low-latency, secure communication over the internet.

Cloudflare's adoption of Rust for this project highlighted Rust's capabilities in the realm of networking and security.

Microsoft: Utilizing Rust in Azure IoT Edge

Microsoft's Azure IoT Edge platform, which enables edge computing for IoT devices, started incorporating Rust into its development stack. Rust's focus on safety and low-level control made it an ideal choice for building components that need to run on resource-constrained devices with high reliability.

By using Rust in Azure IoT Edge, Microsoft aimed to reduce common programming errors that could lead to security vulnerabilities or system crashes. The use of Rust in this context exemplifies the language's versatility in a corporate setting, particularly when dealing with edge computing and IoT solutions.

Figma: Empowering Design Collaboration with Rust

Figma, a web-based design and prototyping tool, turned to Rust to optimize the performance of their collaborative design platform. They identified certain bottlenecks in their existing codebase and rewrote critical components in Rust to improve rendering speed and overall responsiveness.

The transition to Rust allowed Figma to create a more efficient and responsive design tool, enhancing the user experience for millions of designers and collaborators worldwide. Rust's emphasis on performance and safety played a crucial role in achieving these improvements.

These case studies illustrate how Rust has found practical applications in various corporate environments, addressing challenges related to performance, security, and reliability. As Rust continues to gain traction in the industry, it is expected to play an increasingly significant role in corporate software development, particularly in projects where safety and performance are paramount.

Chapter 18: Future Trends and Directions in Rust

Section 18.1: Rust's Roadmap and Future Developments

In this section, we will explore Rust's roadmap and the exciting future developments that are expected to shape the language. Rust has experienced significant growth since its inception, and its development community continues to work on enhancing the language in various ways. Let's delve into some of the key aspects of Rust's future.

1. Stabilization of Features

One of Rust's key principles is stability. The Rust community follows a well-defined process for adding and stabilizing new features. As Rust matures, you can expect more features to become stable, ensuring that the language remains reliable for long-term projects. This stability is essential for corporate environments and production software.

2. Ergonomics and Developer Experience

Rust is committed to improving the developer experience, making it more ergonomic and user-friendly. Future releases are likely to introduce enhancements that simplify common tasks and reduce the learning curve for newcomers. This focus on usability will make Rust even more accessible for developers of all backgrounds.

3. Async/Await and Concurrency

Rust's support for asynchronous programming with `async`/`await` has been a significant development. Future iterations of the language will continue to refine and expand this capability, making it easier to write highly concurrent code. Improved support for concurrency is crucial for building efficient, high-performance systems.

4. Wider Adoption in Systems and Web Development

Rust is already making inroads into systems programming and web development. As the ecosystem continues to grow, you can expect Rust to become a more common choice for building a wide range of applications, from operating systems to web services. Its emphasis on safety and performance makes it well-suited for these domains.

5. Expansion of the Rust Ecosystem

Rust's package manager, Cargo, and the crates ecosystem are central to the language's success. The future will likely bring an expansion of this ecosystem, with more libraries, frameworks, and tools available to Rust developers. This growth will further accelerate Rust's adoption.

6. Integration with Other Languages

Rust's compatibility with other programming languages is a valuable feature. You can anticipate improved integration with languages like C, C++, and Python, making it easier to incorporate Rust into existing codebases and projects.

7. Rust in Education

Rust's approach to safety and system-level programming is garnering attention in educational institutions. The language's pedagogical qualities make it suitable for teaching systems programming and software engineering concepts. Future developments may include more educational resources and initiatives.

8. Community Involvement

Rust's open-source community is a driving force behind its success. Community involvement will remain essential for the language's growth. You can expect more opportunities for participation, contributions, and collaboration in Rust-related projects.

As Rust evolves, its commitment to safety, performance, and developer satisfaction will continue to shape its roadmap. Keeping an eye on Rust's future developments is essential for developers, organizations, and anyone interested in the ever-changing landscape of programming languages. Rust's journey is far from over, and it promises to remain at the forefront of modern software development.

Section 18.2: Emerging Domains and Applications for Rust

In this section, we will explore the emerging domains and applications where Rust is gaining traction. Rust's unique combination of safety, performance, and versatility positions it as a promising language in various fields. Let's delve into some of the exciting areas where Rust is making an impact.

1. WebAssembly (Wasm) Development

Rust is becoming a go-to language for WebAssembly development. WebAssembly allows running high-performance code in web browsers, and Rust's memory safety guarantees make it an excellent choice for writing secure and efficient Wasm modules. Developers are leveraging Rust to build web applications, games, and even blockchain solutions that run directly in the browser.

2. Blockchain and Cryptocurrency

The blockchain industry values security and performance, making Rust an ideal candidate for blockchain development. Several blockchain projects, such as Polkadot and Solana, are built using Rust due to its reliability and low-level control over system resources. Rust is also used for implementing cryptographic algorithms and building secure cryptocurrency-related applications.

3. Embedded Systems and IoT

Rust's focus on memory safety is a significant advantage in the realm of embedded systems and the Internet of Things (IoT). As IoT devices become more prevalent, Rust's ability to prevent memory-related bugs makes it a compelling choice for developing firmware and system software for embedded devices. The language's small footprint and control over hardware are crucial in these resource-constrained environments.

4. Game Development

Rust is gaining popularity in the game development industry. Game engines like Amethyst and Bevy are written in Rust, offering developers a high level of control over their games' performance. Rust's suitability for both game engines and game logic code makes it a versatile option for building interactive and visually appealing games.

5. Machine Learning and Data Science

Rust is making strides in the fields of machine learning and data science. Libraries like ndarray and tangram enable data processing, analysis, and predictive modeling in Rust. While Rust's ecosystem in this domain is still evolving, its performance benefits and safety guarantees are attractive for data-intensive applications.

6. Cloud Computing

As cloud computing continues to grow, Rust is finding its place in this domain. The language's focus on concurrency and performance makes it well-suited for building scalable and responsive cloud services. Rust's small runtime and resource efficiency are advantageous for deploying applications in cloud environments.

7. Networking and Network Services

Rust's robust support for building networked applications and services is gaining attention. Its safety features and low-level control are valuable in implementing networking protocols and ensuring security. Rust is used in network infrastructure, VPN services, and even serverless computing platforms.

8. Quantum Computing

With the emergence of quantum computing, Rust is positioned as a viable language for writing code that interacts with quantum hardware. Its low-level capabilities and safety features are essential in this cutting-edge field, where precise control over hardware is crucial.

Rust's adaptability and suitability for these emerging domains and applications highlight its versatility as a programming language. Developers and organizations looking to stay at the forefront of technology are increasingly turning to Rust to address the unique challenges posed by these fields. Rust's growing ecosystem and community support ensure that it will continue to play a significant role in shaping the future of software development.

Section 18.3: Rust in the Open Source Community

Rust has established a strong presence within the open source community, contributing to and benefiting from the collaborative and transparent nature of open source development. In this section, we will explore Rust's involvement in open source projects, its impact on the community, and the values it shares with the open source ethos.

1. Open Source Roots

Rust itself is an open source project, with its codebase hosted on GitHub. The Rust programming language was built with the open source philosophy in mind, encouraging contributions from developers worldwide. The Rust community actively maintains the language, libraries, and tools, fostering a collaborative environment.

2. Package Management with Cargo

Cargo, Rust's package manager and build tool, has been embraced by the open source community. It simplifies the process of creating, sharing, and using libraries and applications, making it easier for open source developers to distribute their work. Rust's package ecosystem, hosted on crates.io, is a testament to the power of open source collaboration.

3. Contributions to the Wider Open Source Ecosystem

Rust has made substantial contributions to various open source projects beyond its own ecosystem. Its safety and performance benefits have led to the integration of Rust components into software across different domains. For example, Firefox, one of the most popular open source web browsers, incorporates Rust code to enhance security and performance in critical components.

4. Community-Driven Development

Rust's development process is open and community-driven. Decisions about language features, tooling improvements, and library enhancements are made collaboratively. Rust's RFC (Request for Comments) process allows anyone to propose changes or new features, fostering a transparent and inclusive approach to language development.

5. Education and Outreach

Rust's commitment to education aligns with open source values. The Rust community actively creates and maintains educational resources, documentation, and tutorials to make the language accessible to developers of all backgrounds. The Rust Programming Language book, for instance, is available online for free and is a valuable resource for learning Rust.

6. Cross-Project Collaboration

Rust developers frequently collaborate across projects, sharing knowledge and expertise. This cross-project collaboration benefits not only Rust but also the broader open source ecosystem. Developers from different communities can exchange ideas and best practices, leading to improvements in various software projects.

7. Security and Trust

Open source software is often praised for its transparency and security. Rust's emphasis on memory safety and absence of undefined behavior aligns with the open source community's values of building secure and trustworthy software. Rust's compiler acts as a safety net, catching many potential vulnerabilities before code is executed.

8. Community Engagement

Rust's active and welcoming community plays a pivotal role in its success. Community events, conferences, and forums provide opportunities for developers to connect, learn, and collaborate. This sense of belonging and shared purpose is a hallmark of many successful open source projects.

In conclusion, Rust's alignment with open source principles has made it a natural fit within the open source community. Its contributions, collaborative development model, commitment to education, and emphasis on security have solidified Rust's position as a language that embodies the values of open source software. The synergy between Rust and open source continues to drive innovation and advance the state of software development in a transparent and inclusive manner.

Section 18.4: Challenges and Opportunities for Rust

As Rust gains popularity and matures as a programming language, it encounters various challenges and opportunities. In this section, we'll explore some of the key areas where Rust faces both hurdles and possibilities.

1. Learning Curve

Opportunity: Rust's strong emphasis on safety and performance can make it initially challenging for newcomers. However, this also presents an opportunity for developers to enhance their understanding of systems programming, memory management, and safe coding practices. The wealth of educational resources available, such as the Rust Programming Language book and online tutorials, helps ease the learning curve.

2. Library Ecosystem

Challenge: While Rust's ecosystem has grown significantly, it may not yet match the breadth and depth of more established languages. However, this presents an opportunity for developers to contribute by creating and maintaining libraries that fill gaps in the ecosystem. The Rust community actively encourages library development.

3. Adoption in Legacy Codebases

Challenge: Integrating Rust into existing codebases, especially those written in other languages, can be challenging due to differences in memory management and paradigms. However, Rust's Foreign Function Interface (FFI) capabilities allow it to interface with other languages, providing an opportunity for incremental adoption and rewriting critical components in Rust.

4. Tooling

Opportunity: Rust's tooling, including Cargo and rustfmt, has evolved to be user-friendly and productive. However, continuous improvement in developer tools remains an opportunity. The Rust community actively invests in enhancing tooling, making it more efficient and user-friendly.

5. Cross-Platform Development

Opportunity: Rust's suitability for cross-platform development is an advantage. Opportunities exist in leveraging Rust to build applications that run on various operating systems, embedded systems, and the web. Rust's focus on portability and performance positions it as a versatile choice for cross-platform development.

6. Integration with Other Languages

Opportunity: Rust's capability to integrate with other languages presents opportunities for developers to leverage Rust's strengths where it excels, such as systems programming, while using other languages for specific tasks. This integration can lead to more versatile and efficient software solutions.

7. Security and Trust

Opportunity: Rust's memory safety guarantees have the potential to significantly reduce security vulnerabilities in software. Opportunities exist for Rust to continue making strides in the field of security, particularly in critical domains such as cybersecurity and secure systems development.

8. Community Growth

Opportunity: Rust's welcoming and inclusive community is one of its strengths. The opportunity lies in continuing to foster a diverse and global community of contributors, users, and advocates who can collectively drive the language forward and address its challenges.

9. Rust in Emerging Domains

Opportunity: As Rust matures, it has the potential to expand into new domains such as IoT, blockchain, and real-time systems. Developers can explore these emerging areas and leverage Rust's safety and performance advantages to create innovative solutions.

10. Educational Initiatives

Opportunity: Rust's commitment to education is evident through its documentation and learning resources. There is an opportunity to further enhance educational initiatives, making Rust even more accessible to developers at all skill levels.

In conclusion, Rust's journey is marked by both challenges and opportunities. Its unique features, including memory safety, performance, and versatility, position it as a language with tremendous potential. Overcoming challenges while seizing opportunities will continue to shape Rust's evolution and its impact on the world of software development. As Rust continues to grow and evolve, developers, contributors, and the community at large play a pivotal role in its success.

Section 18.5: Preparing for the Future with Rust

As the Rust programming language continues to evolve, developers need to stay informed about future trends and prepare for what lies ahead. In this section, we'll explore strategies for staying ahead of the curve and ensuring that your Rust skills remain relevant in the ever-changing landscape of software development.

1. Continuous Learning

The world of technology evolves rapidly, and Rust is no exception. To prepare for the future, commit to continuous learning. Stay up to date with the latest Rust features, best practices, and community developments. Participate in Rust-related forums, conferences, and workshops to network with fellow developers and learn from their experiences.

2. Contribute to Open Source Projects

Contributing to open source projects is an excellent way to sharpen your Rust skills and gain real-world experience. Open source projects often adopt cutting-edge technologies, and your contributions can make a significant impact. It's also an opportunity to collaborate with experienced developers and learn from their expertise.

3. Explore Emerging Domains

Rust's versatility makes it suitable for various domains, including IoT, blockchain, and real-time systems. Consider exploring these emerging areas to expand your skill set. Building projects in these domains can be a valuable learning experience and may open up new career opportunities.

4. Diversify Your Skill Set

While Rust is a powerful language, it's essential not to limit yourself to a single tool. Diversify your skill set by learning other programming languages and technologies. Familiarity with multiple languages can help you solve a wider range of problems and make you a more versatile developer.

5. Participate in the Rust Community

The Rust community is known for its inclusivity and supportiveness. Engage with the community by joining forums, attending meetups, and contributing to discussions. Collaborating with other Rust enthusiasts can provide insights, mentorship, and a sense of belonging in the developer community.

6. Stay Informed About Rust's Roadmap

Rust's developers maintain a roadmap that outlines the language's future direction and planned features. Keeping an eye on this roadmap can help you anticipate changes and trends in Rust development. You can align your learning and project choices with the language's evolving capabilities.

7. Experiment and Innovate

Rust encourages innovation and experimentation. Don't hesitate to embark on personal projects or experiments to explore Rust's capabilities fully. These projects can lead to breakthroughs, and the experience gained is often transferable to professional work.

8. Mentorship and Teaching

Share your knowledge and expertise by mentoring others or teaching Rust to newcomers. Mentoring and teaching can deepen your understanding of the language and its concepts. It's also a rewarding way to give back to the community and help others prepare for their Rust journey.

9. Adapt to Industry Trends

Stay attuned to broader industry trends in software development. Rust's adoption may grow in specific sectors, so adapt your skill set to meet the demands of industries that increasingly use Rust.

10. Remain Adaptable

Lastly, maintain adaptability as a core skill. The software development landscape is continually changing, and developers who can quickly learn and adapt to new technologies and paradigms will thrive in the future.

In conclusion, preparing for the future with Rust involves a commitment to lifelong learning, active participation in the Rust community, and a willingness to explore new domains and technologies. By staying informed, diversifying your skill set, and embracing change, you can ensure that your Rust skills remain valuable and relevant in the dynamic field of software development.

Chapter 19: Real-World Rust Projects

Section 19.1: Analyzing Open-Source Rust Projects

In this section, we'll delve into the world of open-source Rust projects and explore how you can analyze them to learn from experienced developers, understand best practices, and contribute to the Rust community. Analyzing open-source projects is a fantastic way to gain insights into real-world Rust code and see how different libraries, frameworks, and applications are structured and implemented.

Finding Open-Source Rust Projects

The first step in analyzing open-source Rust projects is to find suitable repositories. Websites like GitHub, GitLab, and Bitbucket host a vast number of open-source projects written in Rust. You can search for Rust projects using keywords, tags, or topics that interest you.

Evaluating Project Relevance

Not all open-source projects will be relevant to your interests or goals. It's essential to evaluate a project's relevance before diving into its codebase. Consider factors such as the project's purpose, size, and activity level. Projects with active maintainers and a community of contributors are often good choices.

Cloning and Exploring Repositories

Once you've identified a project of interest, clone its repository to your local machine using Git. You can explore the codebase using your preferred code editor or IDE. Familiarize yourself with the project's structure, including directories, source files, and build scripts.

Reading Documentation

Many open-source projects provide documentation to help newcomers understand the project's goals, architecture, and codebase. Reading the documentation is a crucial step in gaining insights into the project's design and usage.

Analyzing Code Structure

Pay attention to the project's code structure and organization. Look for common Rust patterns, such as modules, traits, and macros. Analyze how the project manages dependencies, error handling, and concurrency. Understanding these aspects can enhance your Rust programming skills.

Studying Contributions and Pull Requests

Open-source projects often accept contributions from the community in the form of pull requests (PRs). Reviewing accepted PRs and discussions in issues can provide valuable insights into the decision-making process, code reviews, and collaboration within the project.

Running Tests and Benchmarks

Many open-source projects include tests and benchmarks to ensure code correctness and performance. Running these tests locally can help you understand the project's quality standards and performance goals.

Contributing to Projects

After analyzing a project, consider contributing to it. Start with small, well-defined tasks such as fixing bugs or improving documentation. Engaging with the project's community and maintainers is a great way to learn and collaborate.

Tools for Analyzing Rust Projects

Several tools and utilities can assist in analyzing Rust projects. Tools like `cargo`, Rust's package manager, can help you manage dependencies and build projects. Additionally, code analysis tools like `clippy` and `rust-analyzer` can provide valuable feedback on code quality and style.

Learning from Diverse Projects

To gain a broad perspective, explore projects from various domains. Analyze web frameworks, libraries, game engines, system utilities, and more. Each project may introduce you to unique Rust features and design choices.

In conclusion, analyzing open-source Rust projects is an excellent way to learn, improve your coding skills, and contribute to the Rust ecosystem. By exploring diverse projects, studying codebases, and engaging with the community, you can become a more proficient Rust developer and make valuable contributions to the open-source community.

Section 19.2: From Concept to Code: Developing a Rust Project

In this section, we'll explore the process of turning an idea or concept into a tangible Rust project. Whether you're working on a personal project or collaborating with others, understanding the steps involved in project development is crucial for success.

Defining Your Project

Every project begins with an idea or concept. Before writing code, it's essential to define the project's goals, objectives, and scope. Clearly articulate what your project aims to achieve and outline the problem it intends to solve.

Planning and Design

Once you've defined your project's goals, start planning and designing it. Create a high-level project plan that includes milestones, timelines, and tasks. Decide on the project's architecture, data structures, and algorithms. Consider how different components will interact and communicate.

Choosing Dependencies

Rust has a rich ecosystem of libraries and crates that can save you time and effort during development. When starting a new project, choose dependencies wisely. Look for crates that align with your project's requirements and have a track record of active maintenance.

Setting Up the Development Environment

Before you can start writing code, set up your development environment. Install Rust and Cargo, the Rust package manager, on your machine. Create a new Rust project using `cargo new project_name` to generate a project template.

Writing Code

With your project structure in place, begin writing code. Follow Rust's coding conventions and idioms to ensure your code is readable and maintainable. Use Rust's strong type system to catch errors at compile time and minimize runtime issues.

Version Control

Use a version control system like Git to track changes to your project's codebase. Initialize a Git repository in your project directory with `git init` and commit your code regularly. This allows you to collaborate with others, track changes, and easily revert to previous versions if needed.

Testing

Writing tests is a fundamental part of Rust development. Create unit tests and integration tests to ensure your code functions as expected. Rust's built-in testing framework makes it easy to write and run tests.

```rust
#[cfg(test)]
mod tests {
    #[test]
    fn test_addition() {
        assert_eq!(2 + 2, 4);
    }
}
```

Continuous Integration

Set up continuous integration (CI) to automate the process of building, testing, and deploying your project. Services like Travis CI, GitHub Actions, and GitLab CI/CD can run your tests and ensure that your code remains functional as you make changes.

Documentation

Good documentation is essential for your project's users and future contributors. Write clear and concise documentation that explains how to use your project, its API, and any configuration options.

Community and Collaboration

If your project is open-source or collaborative, foster a welcoming and inclusive community. Encourage contributions, respond to issues and pull requests promptly, and follow best practices for maintaining open-source projects.

Security and Maintenance

Regularly update your project's dependencies to address security vulnerabilities and benefit from improvements. Pay attention to security best practices and consider conducting security audits if your project handles sensitive data.

Deployment and Distribution

When your project is ready for release, consider how you will deploy and distribute it. This may involve packaging your project as a crate for others to use or deploying a web application to a hosting service.

Monitoring and Feedback

After releasing your project, monitor its usage and collect feedback from users. This feedback can help you identify areas for improvement and guide future development efforts.

In summary, the process of turning a concept into a Rust project involves defining your project, planning, coding, testing, documenting, and collaborating with others. By following best practices and embracing the Rust community, you can develop successful Rust projects that serve your goals and contribute to the broader Rust ecosystem.

Section 19.3: Project Management for Rust Development

Effective project management is essential for the success of Rust development projects. Whether you're working on a small personal project or a large team endeavor, adopting good project management practices can streamline the development process and ensure that your project meets its goals.

Choosing a Project Management Methodology

There are various project management methodologies to choose from, such as Agile, Scrum, Kanban, and Waterfall. The choice of methodology depends on your project's size, complexity, and requirements. Rust projects often benefit from Agile methodologies that allow for flexibility and adaptation as the project evolves.

Setting Clear Objectives

Define clear and measurable objectives for your Rust project. What do you want to achieve, and how will you measure success? Objectives provide a sense of direction and help prioritize tasks.

Creating a Project Plan

Develop a project plan that outlines the scope of work, timelines, milestones, and deliverables. Consider breaking down the project into smaller tasks and assigning them to team members if you're working in a team. Tools like Gantt charts and project management software can be helpful for visualizing and tracking progress.

Managing Resources

Identify the resources required for your Rust project, including human resources, hardware, software, and budget. Ensure that you have access to the necessary tools and technologies to support development.

Communication and Collaboration

Effective communication is crucial for project success. Maintain clear and open communication channels within your team or with stakeholders. Use collaboration tools like Slack, Microsoft Teams, or project management software to facilitate communication.

Risk Management

Identify potential risks that could impact your Rust project, such as technical challenges, resource constraints, or scope changes. Develop a risk management plan that outlines how you will mitigate and respond to these risks if they occur.

Task Tracking and Progress Monitoring

Use project management tools to track tasks, monitor progress, and identify bottlenecks. Tools like Trello, JIRA, or GitHub Projects can help you visualize the status of tasks and ensure that the project stays on track.

Agile Development Practices

If you're following Agile principles, consider practices like daily stand-up meetings, sprint planning, and backlog grooming. These practices promote transparency, collaboration, and adaptability in your Rust project.

Documentation

Maintain project documentation that includes project requirements, design documents, and coding standards. Documentation helps onboard new team members and ensures that everyone is aligned with project goals.

Quality Assurance

Implement quality assurance practices, including code reviews, automated testing, and continuous integration. These practices help catch and resolve issues early in the development process, improving the overall quality of your Rust project.

Change Management

Be prepared to manage changes to project scope or requirements. Document change requests and evaluate their impact on the project's timeline and budget. Ensure that changes are communicated to all stakeholders.

Project Closure

Once your Rust project is complete, conduct a project closure phase. This includes evaluating project performance, capturing lessons learned, and documenting the final state of the project. Closure ensures that the project is officially concluded and allows for a smooth transition to maintenance or future phases.

In conclusion, effective project management is a critical aspect of Rust development. It helps ensure that your project is completed successfully, on time, and within budget. By adopting the right methodologies and practices, you can maximize the chances of delivering high-quality Rust projects that meet your objectives.

Section 19.4: Rust in Production: Success Stories

Rust has gained popularity for its ability to deliver robust and high-performance applications, and many companies have adopted Rust for their production systems. In this section, we'll explore some success stories of Rust in production environments.

1. Dropbox

Dropbox, a well-known cloud storage and file synchronization service, adopted Rust for its core backend system. Rust's focus on memory safety and system-level programming made it an excellent choice for building critical components of Dropbox's infrastructure. The language's performance and reliability played a crucial role in improving the overall efficiency and stability of Dropbox's services.

2. Mozilla

Mozilla, the organization behind the Firefox web browser, has been a strong supporter of Rust. They've integrated Rust into Firefox to develop parts of the browser's rendering engine and parallel processing components. Rust's safety guarantees helped Mozilla eliminate certain types of security vulnerabilities, making Firefox more secure for its users.

3. Cloudflare

Cloudflare, a provider of content delivery and DDoS protection services, has embraced Rust for building network-related software. Rust's ability to write high-performance, memory-safe code has allowed Cloudflare to develop applications that handle large volumes of network traffic efficiently and securely.

4. Parity Technologies

Parity Technologies is known for its contributions to the Ethereum blockchain ecosystem. They developed the Parity Ethereum client in Rust, which is used by a significant portion of the Ethereum network. Rust's safety features were instrumental in ensuring the reliability and security of this critical piece of blockchain infrastructure.

5. Microsoft

Microsoft has been exploring Rust for system-level programming in certain projects. The company recognizes Rust's potential to improve the security and reliability of its software products. Microsoft's interest in Rust has led to collaborations and contributions to the Rust ecosystem.

6. Figma

Figma, a popular web-based design tool, uses Rust for performance-critical components of its real-time collaboration features. Rust's low-level control and safety features enable Figma to provide a responsive and stable experience to its users, even when editing complex design documents collaboratively.

7. Discord

Discord, a widely used communication platform for gamers, utilizes Rust for building components that require high concurrency and low latency. Rust's ability to manage concurrent operations safely has allowed Discord to scale its real-time chat and voice communication services effectively.

These success stories highlight Rust's versatility and suitability for a wide range of production environments. Whether it's for building web services, browsers, blockchain infrastructure, or cloud-based applications, Rust's focus on safety and performance continues to attract organizations looking to deliver reliable and secure software solutions.

In each of these cases, Rust has demonstrated its value in helping companies achieve their technical and business objectives while maintaining a high level of software quality and security. As Rust's ecosystem continues to grow, more organizations are likely to explore its benefits and consider it for their production projects.

Section 19.5: Learning from Real-World Rust Applications

Learning from real-world Rust applications can provide valuable insights into best practices, design patterns, and strategies for building robust software. In this section, we'll explore the importance of studying existing Rust projects and highlight some key takeaways.

1. Code Readability

One of the first things you'll notice when examining real-world Rust codebases is the emphasis on code readability. Rust developers often follow consistent naming conventions, use meaningful variable and function names, and provide thorough comments and documentation. This focus on clarity makes it easier for both the original authors and other contributors to understand and maintain the code over time.

2. Safety and Concurrency

Rust's ownership system and type system are central to its design philosophy. Real-world projects demonstrate how these features are used to ensure memory safety and prevent data races in concurrent code. By studying how Rust projects handle ownership, borrowing, and lifetimes, you can gain a deeper understanding of how to write safe and concurrent code.

3. Error Handling

Effective error handling is crucial for building reliable software. Rust's Result and Option types, along with the match and unwrap constructs, are commonly used for error handling. Real-world Rust applications showcase various error-handling strategies, including custom error types, error chaining, and comprehensive error messages. Learning from these examples can help you improve your own error-handling practices.

4. Testing and Documentation

Rust projects often prioritize testing and documentation. You'll find extensive test suites that cover different aspects of the codebase, ensuring that changes don't introduce regressions. Additionally, comprehensive documentation, both in code comments and external documentation files, makes it easier for developers to understand how to use and contribute to the project.

5. Dependency Management

Dependency management is a critical aspect of any software project. Real-world Rust projects demonstrate how to define and manage dependencies using Cargo, Rust's package manager. You can learn about best practices for specifying dependencies, handling version constraints, and dealing with build scripts and custom build logic.

6. Design Patterns and Architectural Choices

Every software project makes design decisions, and Rust projects are no exception. By studying different Rust applications, you can gain insights into various design patterns and architectural choices. You'll see how projects organize their code into modules, handle state management, and implement common software engineering principles.

7. Performance Optimization

Rust is known for its emphasis on performance, and real-world applications often contain optimizations for both CPU and memory usage. Examining how Rust projects optimize their code, use data structures efficiently, and minimize allocations can teach you valuable performance-oriented programming techniques.

8. Community and Collaboration

Many Rust projects are open source and benefit from contributions from a global community of developers. Studying these projects can provide valuable lessons in collaborative software development. You can learn how to use version control systems effectively, manage issues and pull requests, and foster a welcoming and inclusive community around your own projects.

In conclusion, real-world Rust applications serve as a rich source of knowledge and inspiration for Rust developers of all levels. By exploring existing projects, you can learn from the experiences of others, adopt best practices, and gain a deeper understanding of Rust's unique features and capabilities. Whether you're a beginner or an experienced Rustacean, studying real-world code can help you become a more proficient Rust programmer and contribute to the growing Rust ecosystem.

Chapter 20: Concluding Rust Journey

Section 20.1: Best Practices in Rust Programming

As we conclude this comprehensive journey through Rust programming, it's essential to emphasize best practices that can help you write high-quality, maintainable, and efficient Rust code. These practices encapsulate the collective wisdom of the Rust community and can serve as valuable guidelines for your future projects.

1. Code Readability and Clarity

One of Rust's strengths is its readability. Always write code that is easy for others (and your future self) to understand. Follow consistent naming conventions, use meaningful variable and function names, and provide clear comments and documentation. Code readability is the foundation of maintainable software.

2. Embrace Rust's Ownership System

Rust's ownership system is a powerful tool for memory safety and concurrency. Embrace it fully by understanding ownership, borrowing, and lifetimes. Avoid unnecessary cloning and use references where appropriate. Leverage Rust's unique features to write safe and efficient code.

3. Error Handling

Effective error handling is essential for robust software. Utilize Rust's `Result` and `Option` types for explicit error handling. Consider custom error types when necessary, and provide informative error messages. Always handle errors gracefully rather than using `unwrap` excessively.

4. Comprehensive Testing

Testing is a fundamental part of Rust development. Write thorough test suites to cover different code paths and ensure that your code behaves as expected. Automated testing helps catch regressions and build confidence in your code's correctness.

5. Documentation

Document your code comprehensively. Use doc comments (`///`) to provide clear explanations of functions, types, and modules. External documentation is also essential for users and contributors. Rust's built-in tools make generating and publishing documentation straightforward.

6. Dependency Management with Cargo

Cargo, Rust's package manager, simplifies dependency management. Always specify dependencies accurately, follow semantic versioning (semver), and keep dependencies up to date. Pay attention to build scripts and custom build logic when needed.

7. Design Patterns and Architecture

Choose appropriate design patterns and architectural styles for your projects. Organize your code into modules and structures that make sense for your application. Consider separation of concerns and maintainability when designing your software.

8. Performance Optimization

Rust excels in performance, but optimization should be based on profiling and benchmarking. Identify bottlenecks and use Rust's features to optimize code carefully. Avoid premature optimization, and remember that readability and maintainability should not be sacrificed for minor performance gains.

9. Open Source Contribution and Collaboration

Consider contributing to open source projects and collaborating with other developers. Version control systems like Git are essential tools for collaborative development. Create welcoming and inclusive communities around your projects to foster collaboration.

10. Lifelong Learning

Rust is a rapidly evolving language, and the ecosystem is continuously growing. Keep learning by exploring new libraries, tools, and language features. Stay engaged with the Rust community through forums, conferences, and online resources.

In conclusion, Rust is a versatile and powerful language with a vibrant community and ecosystem. By following these best practices, you can make the most of Rust's unique features and build software that is not only reliable and efficient but also a pleasure to work with. Your journey with Rust doesn't end here; it's just the beginning of a rewarding programming experience.

Section 20.2: The Rust Community and Continuing Education

The Rust programming language has gained a reputation not only for its technical excellence but also for its strong and welcoming community. In this section, we'll explore the significance of the Rust community and how you can continue your education and growth as a Rust programmer.

The Rust Community

The Rust community is known for its inclusivity, friendliness, and willingness to help newcomers. Whether you're a beginner or an experienced developer, you'll find support and camaraderie within the Rust ecosystem. Here are some aspects of the Rust community that you should be aware of:

1. Online Forums and Social Media

Platforms like the official Rust forum, Reddit's /r/rust, and the Rust subreddit are excellent places to ask questions, seek advice, and engage in discussions with fellow Rustaceans. Twitter also has an active Rust community, and you can follow Rust-related hashtags to stay updated.

2. Conferences and Meetups

Rust has a strong presence at tech conferences and meetups worldwide. Events like RustConf, RustFest, and local Rust meetups provide opportunities to connect with Rust enthusiasts, attend talks, and participate in workshops.

3. Open Source Collaboration

Rust's ecosystem thrives on open source contributions. You can actively contribute to Rust projects, libraries, and tools. Many open source projects in Rust welcome new contributors, making it an ideal way to gain practical experience and give back to the community.

4. Learning Resources

The Rust community has created numerous learning resources, including books, tutorials, video courses, and documentation. Many of these resources are freely available online and cater to learners of all levels.

Continuing Your Education

Rust's ecosystem and the software development field, in general, are continually evolving. To stay relevant and maximize your Rust programming skills, consider the following strategies:

1. Explore Advanced Topics

As you become more proficient in Rust, explore advanced topics such as metaprogramming, unsafe Rust, and custom data structures. These areas can empower you to tackle complex projects and optimize your code further.

2. Follow the Rust Roadmap

Stay informed about Rust's official roadmap and the language's future direction. Rust's development is guided by a well-defined process, and understanding where the language is heading can help you align your learning goals.

3. Contribute to Open Source

Contributing to open source projects not only enhances your programming skills but also strengthens your ties to the Rust community. Look for projects that align with your interests and skill level, and be an active participant.

4. Attend Rust Events

Participate in Rust-related events, both online and in person. These events offer opportunities to learn from experts, network with other developers, and gain insights into the latest trends and best practices.

5. Experiment and Build

Apply your Rust knowledge by working on personal projects or exploring new domains. Whether it's game development, web applications, system tools, or embedded systems, hands-on experience is invaluable for growth.

6. Collaborate and Mentor

Collaborate with other Rust developers on projects or mentor newcomers to the language. Teaching others is a powerful way to solidify your own understanding and give back to the community.

In conclusion, your Rust journey doesn't end with this book. The Rust community is an excellent resource for ongoing learning and collaboration. By staying engaged, exploring advanced topics, and contributing to open source, you can continue to thrive as a Rust programmer and be part of an exciting and dynamic community. Rust's future is bright, and your role in it can be as impactful as you choose to make it.

Section 20.3: Future-Proofing Your Rust Skills

As a Rust programmer, one of the key considerations for your career is to future-proof your skills. The technology landscape is ever-changing, and staying relevant is essential for long-term success. In this section, we'll discuss strategies for ensuring that your Rust skills remain valuable in the years to come.

Embrace Lifelong Learning

The first and most crucial step in future-proofing your Rust skills is to embrace the concept of lifelong learning. The software development field evolves rapidly, and new technologies, libraries, and paradigms emerge regularly. Rust, as a language known for its focus on safety, performance, and productivity, is no exception. To keep your skills up to date, make learning a continuous part of your professional life.

Here are some ways to approach lifelong learning:

1. Stay Updated on Rust

Rust's development is ongoing, with new features, enhancements, and improvements being introduced regularly. Follow the official Rust blog, mailing lists, and release notes to stay informed about the latest developments in the language.

2. Explore Related Technologies

Rust often intersects with other technologies and ecosystems, such as WebAssembly, embedded systems, and cloud computing. Expanding your knowledge in these areas can complement your Rust skills and open up new opportunities.

3. Invest in Advanced Topics

Delve into advanced Rust topics like metaprogramming, unsafe Rust, and compiler plugins. These areas can provide you with a deeper understanding of the language and enable you to solve complex problems more effectively.

Diversify Your Skill Set

While Rust is a powerful language, it's not the only tool in your developer toolbox. Diversifying your skill set can make you a more versatile and adaptable programmer. Consider learning other programming languages and technologies to broaden your horizons.

1. Learn Other Languages

Exploring languages like Python, JavaScript, Go, or C++ can expose you to different programming paradigms and use cases. Each language has its strengths and weaknesses, and understanding them can help you choose the right tool for a given task.

2. Master Software Development Practices

In addition to language-specific skills, focus on mastering software development practices such as version control, testing, debugging, and project management. These skills are transferable and valuable across various programming languages.

Build a Strong Portfolio

Your portfolio of projects and contributions is a tangible representation of your skills and expertise. Continuously working on projects, whether personal or open source, can showcase your abilities to potential employers or collaborators.

1. Personal Projects

Create and maintain personal projects that interest you. Building applications, libraries, or tools in Rust allows you to apply what you've learned and demonstrate your problem-solving abilities.

2. Open Source Contributions

Contributing to open source projects not only gives back to the community but also exposes you to real-world codebases and collaborative development. It can be an excellent way to learn from experienced developers and showcase your contributions to a wider audience.

Stay Adaptable and Resilient

In the fast-paced world of technology, adaptability and resilience are essential qualities. Be prepared to pivot, learn new skills, and adapt to changing circumstances. Rust's strong focus on safety and performance equips you with problem-solving and critical-thinking skills that can be applied in various domains.

Networking and Collaboration

Networking is a valuable aspect of future-proofing your career. Connect with other Rust developers, attend conferences and meetups, and engage in online forums and communities. Collaborating with peers can lead to new opportunities, insights, and knowledge sharing.

In conclusion, future-proofing your Rust skills involves a combination of continuous learning, diversifying your skill set, building a strong portfolio, staying adaptable, and networking. The software development landscape is dynamic, and your ability to evolve with it will determine your long-term success as a Rust programmer. By staying curious, embracing change, and actively participating in the Rust community, you can ensure that your skills remain relevant and valuable throughout your career.

Section 20.4: The Impact of Rust on Software Development

Rust has had a significant impact on the landscape of software development since its inception. In this section, we'll explore the ways in which Rust has influenced the industry and why it's considered a game-changer in several areas.

1. Memory Safety and Systems Programming

Rust's emphasis on memory safety without sacrificing performance has revolutionized systems programming. Historically, C and C++ were the go-to languages for system-level development, but they came with a high risk of memory-related bugs like null pointer dereferences and buffer overflows. Rust addresses these issues at compile-time, making it a safer choice for developing critical systems and applications.

2. Concurrency and Parallelism

In the era of multi-core processors, writing concurrent and parallel code is essential for harnessing the full power of modern hardware. Rust's ownership system and strict rules ensure thread safety without the need for locks and mutexes. This makes concurrent programming more accessible, less error-prone, and efficient.

3. Web Assembly (Wasm) and Browser-Based Applications

Rust's ability to compile to WebAssembly has opened up new possibilities for running high-performance code in web browsers. Developers can write computationally intensive applications in Rust and execute them securely and efficiently in web environments. This capability has accelerated the adoption of Rust in web development.

4. Security and Safe Systems

Rust's design prevents common security vulnerabilities like buffer overflows and data races. This is especially crucial in security-critical applications, including operating systems, network services, and cryptographic software. Rust's adoption in these domains has improved the overall security posture of software systems.

5. Language Design and Innovation

Rust's development process, driven by the Rust community and supported by Mozilla, has become a model for open-source language design. It showcases the benefits of strong community involvement, rigorous governance, and a focus on user needs. Rust's innovations, such as the ownership system and pattern matching, have influenced other programming languages.

6. Growing Ecosystem and Libraries

Rust's ecosystem has expanded significantly, with a growing number of libraries, frameworks, and tools. This growth has made Rust a viable choice for a wide range of applications, from web development to game development, and from system utilities to cloud services.

7. Education and Learning

Rust's emphasis on correctness and safety has made it an excellent language for teaching programming and systems concepts. It has been used in educational settings to introduce students to low-level programming without exposing them to the pitfalls of languages like C and C++.

8. Community and Collaboration

Rust's community is known for its inclusivity, diversity, and commitment to helping newcomers. The Rust community actively encourages collaboration and knowledge sharing, fostering an environment where developers can learn and grow together.

In conclusion, Rust has made a substantial impact on software development by addressing critical issues related to memory safety, concurrency, security, and language design. Its influence extends to various domains, including systems programming, web development, and education. As Rust continues to evolve and gain momentum, its impact on the industry is likely to grow, making it a valuable language for both developers and organizations seeking reliable and secure software solutions.

Section 20.5: Final Thoughts and Next Steps in Rust Programming

As we conclude this book, it's essential to reflect on your journey in learning Rust and consider the next steps in your Rust programming adventure. Rust is a versatile and powerful language with a growing community and an exciting future. Here are some final thoughts and recommendations to guide you further:

1. Master the Fundamentals

Before diving into advanced topics, ensure you have a solid understanding of Rust's fundamentals. This includes ownership, borrowing, lifetimes, and common data structures. A strong foundation will make it easier to tackle complex problems and optimize your code.

2. Explore Specialized Domains

Rust's versatility allows you to explore various domains such as systems programming, web development, game development, and more. Consider which areas interest you the most and start building projects in those domains. Practical experience is invaluable for mastering Rust.

3. Contribute to Open Source

Contributing to open-source Rust projects is an excellent way to learn from experienced developers, gain visibility in the Rust community, and give back to the ecosystem. Whether it's fixing bugs, improving documentation, or adding features, there are plenty of opportunities to get involved.

4. Stay Informed

Rust is an evolving language with regular releases and updates. Stay informed about Rust's latest developments by following the official Rust blog, participating in community forums, and attending Rust conferences and meetups. Keeping up to date will ensure you're aware of new features and best practices.

5. Experiment with Advanced Features

As you become more comfortable with Rust, don't hesitate to experiment with advanced features like macros, metaprogramming, and unsafe code. These features can unlock new possibilities and improve your productivity.

6. Continue Learning

Learning Rust is an ongoing process. There are plenty of resources available, including books, online courses, and documentation. Consider exploring topics like advanced concurrency, networking, cryptography, and more to deepen your knowledge.

7. Collaborate and Network

Rust's community is known for its friendliness and willingness to help. Collaborate with other Rustaceans on projects, ask questions, and share your experiences. Networking can lead to valuable insights, partnerships, and career opportunities.

8. Teach and Mentor

Sharing your knowledge of Rust with others is a rewarding experience. Consider mentoring beginners, giving talks or workshops, or writing tutorials. Teaching can solidify your understanding of Rust and contribute to its growth.

9. Embrace Challenges

Rust's focus on safety and correctness may present challenges, especially when transitioning from dynamically typed languages. Embrace these challenges as opportunities for growth and learning. Overcoming them will make you a better programmer overall.

10. Enjoy the Journey

Learning Rust is not just about reaching a destination; it's about enjoying the journey. Rust offers unique insights into programming and software development. Take time to appreciate the beauty of Rust and the sense of accomplishment it brings.

In closing, Rust is a language that rewards perseverance and curiosity. It empowers you to build reliable, efficient, and secure software. Whether you're a beginner or an experienced developer, Rust has something to offer. So, continue your Rust programming journey with enthusiasm, and remember that the Rust community is here to support you along the way. Happy coding!

www.ingramcontent.com/pod-product-compliance
Lightning Source LLC
LaVergne TN
LVHW052057060326
832903LV00061B/3296